# Reviews

*After applying the strategies in this book, my baby went from only sleeping 10-minute stretches during the day and one-hour stretches at night at a time to sleeping two-hour stretches during the day and 11 hours straight at night.*

A mom, Twila Yoder

*My name is Tommy Spears. I am a dentist in Maryville, Tennessee. I've treated approximately 8000 infants and toddlers for assessments of oral tethered issues as it pertains to breast and or bottle-feeding for over 10 years now. Beth Miller's book, "Why Some Babies Do Not Sleep Well" has a bevy of information to help parents with their newborns and also has great information for their child as they grow and develop properly. I appreciate her emphasis on proper breast/bottle feeding, which is paramount in my opinion to start life with the greatest advantage. Thank you, Beth, for your contribution in this field!*

Tommy Spears DDS FOM

Crestview Dental Care

# Why Some Babies Do Not Sleep Well

## How To Fix your Newborn To 6 Month Baby's Sleep Problems For Good

BETH MILLER

If you have any questions or comments, you may reach me at
bethmiller90@protonmail.com.


Front cover image from Freepik.com
Cover design by Mari Jean Royal
Editor, Tabitha Schmidt
Book formatting, Anita Otto

# Dedication

I DEDICATE THIS BOOK to my husband, **Mahlon,** the love of my life, who learned all these lessons with me while raising our babies.

I also dedicate this book to **Dr. Mahoney of Mahoney Family Dentistry.** What a hero you have been to us and many others! After hearing over and over, my baby did not have a lip tie, you were the first person who gave me hope. You took one look and confirmed what I felt all along. My baby DID HAVE a lip tie, and that WAS causing her discomfort. Her discomfort that I was told I 'imagined.' Your compassion for babies (and parents!) is commendable.

And to all the dentists out there who perform frenectomies. You are also a hero; correcting a baby's mouth tie after a mom has been repeatedly told, "Your baby is fine," when a mom can tell HER BABY IS NOT FINE. You don't just resolve an infant's pain and discomfort—you save a mom's sanity.

And for all the moms spending sleepless nights, looking for answers for their babies. Your undying efforts at ministering to your baby reveal your heart of love and kindness.

# Acknowledgements

Thanks to the following individuals who have helped immensely with this book.

Dr. Lawrence Kotlow, you were so generous in allowing me to use your information.

Dr Eilish Welsh, how can I thank you enough for all your input to make this book possible. Not only that, the many times you willingly take time off your busy schedule to answer all my questions about tongue ties. All the babies (and moms!) that have come to me and experienced a transformation in their sleep are a direct reflection of your invaluable counsel and guidance. Your team at Brunswick kidds is amazing and I value your insight immensely.

Dr. Cockley of East Berlin Smiles, your contribution was greatly appreciated.

# Contents

Introduction   IX

1. Why Won't My Baby Sleep?   1

2. The 4 Biggest Causes for Sleep Issues in a Baby   2

3. The Overstimulation Factor   9

4. Defining An Overtired Baby   19

5. The Importance of Routine and Habit   23

6. Troubleshooting   37

7. Routine Changes   76

8. Tips To Lessen Teething And/or Flu Symptoms   82

9. The Effects of Tongue and Lip Ties   92

10. What Is a Lip and Tongue Tie?   94

11. Maternal Effects of a Tongue/Lip Tie   97

12. Infant's Effects of a Tongue/Lip Tie   99

13. Cheek Ties   116

14. Who Can Correct A Tongue And Lip Tie?   117

15. Testimonials   120

Final Thoughts   127

Note From The Author   128

Dentists Who Perform Frenectomies, Lactation Con-          137
sultants, Cranial Therapists

Resources                                                 172

Notes                                                     179

Also by Beth Miller                                       180

# Introduction

BECOMING A PARENT CAN be daunting. Very daunting. I remember after I married but didn't have any children yet and I was talking to one of my friends who had a baby. I remember asking her how in the world she knew how to be a mom and take care of her baby. Back then, I could not imagine how you could know what your baby wants if she couldn't talk. I smile as I think back to that conversation. Yes, it can be overwhelming, and many times I have wondered what could be wrong with my baby. That's why I wrote this book. Not because I have motherhood all figured out. Instead, my prayer is that this information could help other moms understand their baby's needs.

Being a mom is exhausting. Not only are you your baby's primary caretaker, you have meals to make, a house to keep clean, besides many other responsibilities. Having a baby who cannot sleep well adds even more pressure to a mom. If a baby is not sleeping well, neither is mom! Then a mom becomes even more exhausted and questions, why doesn't my baby sleep well? Why have catnaps become the norm for my baby? Hopefully, this book will help you find answers to your baby's inability to sleep. Since you are looking for solutions, we will get right into it.

# CHAPTER 1

# Why Won't My Baby Sleep?

BRINGING A BABY INTO the world is a life-changing event. Suddenly, you are in charge of a little human. This is both exhilarating and overwhelming. It's exciting that the baby is truly yours, but also overwhelming considering the extra responsibilities.

The addition of a new baby can present many challenges. One very common challenge is getting a baby to sleep well. A mom needs her sleep in order to function. However, if the baby is not sleeping, neither is the mother.

Thankfully, there are many solutions in this book that will guide you on your quest for a baby that sleeps well. It may take a little troubleshooting as you decipher which methods and ideas will work for you and your baby. You bought this book because you obviously want solutions. So, let's go!

# CHAPTER 2

# The 4 Biggest Causes for Sleep Issues in a Baby

So, WHAT CAUSES SLEEP issues in a baby? This is a great question, and if I can help you answer this question, I can help you get better sleep before your baby. Here is why. There are some common denominators no matter what sleep issues you want to resolve. This could be your baby has a hard time falling asleep or staying asleep during the day. This could mean your baby is waking up often at night and you wish to resolve this. So, let's look at some of the common issues that cause sleep problems.

**Cause No. 1. You are not regulating your baby's nervous system, causing overstimulation.**

You may have been told to implement an eat, play, sleep routine, and this is detrimental to helping a baby's nervous system calm down before bedtime if your baby is a newborn. Or you may simply not know anything about the eat, play, sleep routine, but you are still overstimulating your baby before bedtime. We will look at this in *The Overstimulation Factor* chapter.

**Cause No. 2. You have not implemented a routine from day 1 to help your baby form good sleep habits.**

So, this goes hand-in-hand with regulating your baby's nervous system, and that is implementing a consistent routine. A newborn baby is a creature of habit; after you have done something three times in a row, they will expect that. In addition, newborn babies up to the age of six weeks are really sleepy. If you want to teach your baby good sleep habits, it is critical to implement them in the first six weeks. The problem is too many moms wait until their baby is three months or older and already has sleep issues. Finally, they are desperate for peace and decide to sleep train. Then there is going to be a lot of crying as a baby tries to unlearn the sleep habits you have helped them form.So, the longer you wait to teach your baby good sleep habits, the more your baby is going to cry.

It's like this: what if you taught your 7-year-old daughter that 1+1 = 5? Then, four months later, you would teach her that 1+1 is actually two. Of course, your daughter is going to be confused. Now she doesn't know what to believe. This is the same thing that happens with babies when we don't follow a specific routine and help them form good sleep habits from day one. Suddenly your baby has poor sleep habits and cannot even fall asleep without you feeding, rocking or bouncing them constantly, and this is exhausting for a mom. As you try to teach your baby new habits, your baby is bewildered and confused because they never had the chance to fall asleep independently in the crib before. It's like for the first three months they were fed, rocked or bounced to sleep and now suddenly one day they have to learn to fall asleep independently. Therefore, there is always a lot of crying involved with sleep training because the baby is bewildered and is trying to figure out what is required of her.

The same is true for contact naps. It's okay to do a contact nap occasionally, but if you do it all the time, your baby is going to think that this is the way to do it and will take that as a habit. Suddenly one day, Mom is overwhelmed, because baby will **only** fall asleep on her. Now we have a problem because baby doesn't want to sleep in the crib, and now mom doesn't get any sleep.

It is **much easier** to teach your baby good sleep habits in the first six weeks than it is to wait until your baby is three months old or older and then attempt to sleep train. There's also a lot more crying if you wait. In fact, the older your child is before you teach her good sleep habits, the more crying there is going to be. That is because the more often you teach a child something, the more they will internalize it, and the harder it will be for them to unlearn it. So here's my advice: **don't start what you don't intend to keep doing.** Do you want to keep doing contact naps? If you do that, that is okay, but a lot of moms don't realize that they are teaching their babies poor sleep habits, and they wish they had never started. Like I said, some contact naps are okay, like say, for example, your baby is sick, and you rock your baby to sleep and cuddle them — that is okay. The problem is, if you are doing it for every nap every day that it turns into a bad habit.

**Cause No. 3. Not teaching your baby to fall asleep in the crib from day one.**

This also goes hand-in-hand with teaching your baby a good routine. So, here is what a lot of moms will do; they will either feed, rock or bounce their baby to sleep. Then, they will try to transfer their baby to the crib, hoping the baby stays asleep. If the baby stays asleep after they have transferred the baby, good, if not, they have to start the entire process over again.

Here is a big problem with this. Your baby is going to wake up and does not know when or how she got in the crib. This is startling for a baby to wake up and not know where she is and how she got there. It makes a baby feel tricked and abandoned. Babies don't like "tricks." Now your baby is going to wake up and wonder what happened, and it creates an insecurity in the baby. It's like this—how secure would you feel if you woke up one morning and you did not know where you were and how you got there? What if you fell asleep in your bed and woke up in a motel bed that's unfamiliar with no knowledge of how you got there? **The problem with this tactic is one day the trick is on you**, and you can't even put your baby down because baby doesn't like to wake up feeling tricked and dumped. This can lead to catnaps and constant night wakings because the baby wakes up and feels startled to be in a different place than she was in when she fell asleep. Then the baby realizes she's no longer in your arms, and she feels forsaken and dumped. Then she is going to cry, and you're going to have to go in constantly and rock her back to sleep or feed or whatever you did to help her fall asleep in the first place.

In the same way, if you are only doing contact sleep, or co-sleeping and suddenly you need to go eat or go to the restroom and you can barely sneak away because your baby will wake up, it's because your baby doesn't like to be tricked. It is much better to help your baby fall asleep in the same place and in the same way that you actually want them to sleep long term than try to do transferring or sneaking away. This practice creates insecurity in a baby. Like I said, you can trick them now, but in a couple of months, the trick will be on you, and you will have a Velcro baby that doesn't want to let you out of their sight, especially to sleep. This is how a baby learns to hate bedtime—Mom makes a game out of it. The baby catches on after a while, and then Mom is caught in a losing battle that she created. This creates exhaustion for both mom and baby.

Most moms are really concerned about wanting a secure attachment with their baby. Most moms are shocked and surprised when

I tell them that by NOT teaching their baby good sleep habits, they are actually creating an insecure baby. Therefore, babies cry at naptime simply because they feel insecure about being put down for a nap because they don't know what to expect. So here is my advice: **teach your baby what you want them to know right away because you're going to have a more secure baby.** That way, baby feels you are dependable and stick to your word. If your baby feels like you're going to do one thing one day and then have a different rule or routine for the next, she's going to feel you are wishy-washy. Babies want security and routine, and consistency builds that security.

Most moms are not aware of how incredibly smart their babies are. You give a baby a consistent routine, and they know exactly what to expect every time. The result is a secure, cheerful baby who enjoys nap time. In fact, my 2-year-old will either take a nap herself sometimes by lying on the floor with her blanket and simply falling asleep or she will ask me to put her in her bed for a nap. No fuss, no whining. This is because from day one there were no games played with her ever. She either fell asleep independently or I stroked her head as she was falling asleep in her crib from day one. Since bedtime was built around making her feel secure, there was little to no crying from day one. As a result, there were no bad sleep habits formed and no bad habits to break.

Now every baby's temperament is different, and some babies might be fine co-sleeping or contact napping or even being transferred all the time, and they still sleep well. Some babies have poor sleep habits from the get-go, and yet they grow out of it. However, I recommend following a specific routine and helping your baby form good sleep habits from day one because I see so many babies that are six months, 12 months and even older, who still do not sleep through the night simply because mama didn't implement good sleep habits from day one. As the saying goes, *prepare and prevent rather than repair and repent.*

## Cause No. 4. Tongue, lip, and cheek ties

I am seeing more and more babies that are not sleeping well, especially at night because they have a tongue and or lip tie. Therefore, I feel it is crucial to help moms understand the symptoms that are behind the ties. Catnaps are also very common in babies who have ties. The last part of this book will explain all of this. Because of the number of babies that I have worked with that have undiagnosed ties, I recommend you don't miss that, because **until underlying ties are addressed, your baby won't be able to sleep well no matter what you do. Nothing else in this book will work to help your baby sleep well if your baby has a mouth tie.** Even a "small" tie. So many moms are told by "professionals" that it's just a small tie, nothing to worry about. This is an enormous problem because usually the practitioner telling you this doesn't understand how a "small tie" can cause a BIG problem!

It is critical that if your baby has a tie that your baby is evaluated by a knowledgeable professional. I have had so many moms come to me, and, their baby had a tie, but they told me that their pediatrician, doctor, dentist, lactation consultant, midwife or chiropractor, or any other medical professional said their baby does not have a tie or their baby has a tie and it's not causing issues. However, once I send them to someone with specific training in identifying and correcting ties, and the tie is **correctly revised** (lots of ties are missed or baby had an incomplete procedure because of lack of knowledge on the practitioner's part), the sleep issues resolve on their own. Since working with babies, I have found this to be the **biggest cause of sleep issues in babies.** This includes catnaps, night wakings, and baby fighting bedtime. Sometimes all Mom has to do is go to a knowledgeable professional and get this corrected, and *boom!* sleep issues stop cold turkey. No change in sleep routine. That is because ties make a baby uncomfortable and inhibits their breathing. This makes it impossible for the baby to sleep well. **No sleep routine can ever fix a baby's sleep until a skilled professional corrects the ties. Period**. Since so many babies have slept better so quickly after I helped mom find a specialist to correct this, I now address this problem before addressing anything else. It is the biggest game changer to any sleep program. Head to Chapter 9 to learn more.

# CHAPTER 3

# The Overstimulation Factor

THE FIRST REASON YOUR baby might not sleep well could be because of something I call the overstimulation factor. More stimulation than a baby's underdeveloped nervous system can handle can cause overstimulation. An overstimulated baby cannot sleep well.

Often, babies who cannot sleep are also fussy. That is because they are overstimulated. Overstimulation makes a baby cry as she tries to release the tension from all the overexcitement. The result will be a baby who cries and cannot sleep.

Imagine a scene with me: A newborn baby wakes up in the morning, and the mother retrieves the baby from the crib. She talks to the baby and then feeds the baby—either nursing or giving a bottle. After that, she burps the baby. Next, she changes the baby's diaper. While changing the baby's diaper, she continues talking to the baby. Then she places her in a swing. Soon, the baby cries, and the mom picks up the baby and talks to her more. Next, she tries rocking the baby while continuing to talk to the baby. The baby cries while the mother continues trying to shush her, causing the baby to cry even more. When she is finally able to get the baby to sleep, the baby sleeps only a couple of minutes before waking again.

The problem in the above scenario is that there is too much stimulation going on for a newborn baby to handle. The younger a baby is, the less stimulation their immature nervous system can handle. Infants younger than four months cannot tolerate much interaction. If a baby, especially an infant under four months, has too much stimulation during the day, not only will she be fussy and unable to sleep during the day, but by evening she will be inconsolable. Then, she will cry for hours, trying to release the pent-up and overwhelmed feelings caused by overstimulation during the day. Of course, your baby will not sleep if she is crying excessively from overstimulation.

To prevent overstimulating your baby, you need to understand the sources of stimulation.

**Sources of Stimulation for a Baby**:

1. Screen time/blue light exposure

2. Musical and/or flashing toys

3. Brightly colored toys and colors

4. Jostling or fast movement

5. Baby swings

6. Diaper changing

7. Bathing

8. Changing their clothes

9. Burping, specifically patting to burp

10. Loud noises

11. Unfamiliar people and/or places

12.  Excessively talking to them.

Blue light will overstimulate your baby and hinder their sleep. Therefore, you should not expose your baby to any devices that emit blue light. Cell phones, laptops, and TVs all emit blue light. Even the dashboard of your vehicle has blue lighting. This is so drivers can stay awake when driving at night. Your baby's eyes are less effective at blocking blue light than your own, meaning even a brief exposure can disrupt their sleep schedule. I have the blue light on my phone turned way down. However, I still try to keep my phone screen facing down at all times, especially when my baby is around. There are videos online to show you how to turn your blue light down on your phone.

Screen time is very detrimental to your baby's development, especially a very young baby. Additionally, videos are way too stimulating for a baby. There are so many things happening on the screen at once and a baby cannot process that.

Some sources of stimulation are inevitable, such as changing your baby's diaper. However, the mother was most likely doing a lot of talking to the baby and not reading the baby's cues.

Since a baby's nervous system is still underdeveloped, when you talk to a newborn baby, they will look away after a bit. This is the baby's way of saying, "This is enough engagement for me now. Please respect my limits." You need to wait until your baby looks back at you again and then you can continue talking to her. If she does not look back at you, this is your sign to stop talking to her. If you continue talking, it will be too much stimulation for a baby's immature nervous system to handle.

However, let's say you talk to your baby and she looks away, so you stop talking. Then she looks back at you, and the cycle continues repeatedly. This can overstimulate the baby if overdone. Babies only have a limited amount of energy and attention span for talking and engagement from you, and then it will turn to overstimulation quickly.

The point is to engage with your baby only at the level that they can handle for their age. Infants from newborn to four months old are the most easily overstimulated. Sometimes newborns just want eye contact, not interaction. Maintaining steady eye contact seems comforting for a newborn, and this is a great way to bond with them.

If you want to talk or sing to your baby, you can do it before feeding. Later, I will explain why it is important to engage with your baby, preferably before feeding, if your baby is under four months old.

Babies from newborn to about four months old do not want or need any sort of toys. Anything bright and flashy is too overstimulating; anything that plays music or flashes is just too much for them to process.

I recommend holding your baby calmly and not swinging him around much. That is why baby swings can be so overstimulating, because the swing is moving so quickly. Baby swings that rock from side to side can be horribly stimulating.

Any fast movement is a no-no. If you rock your baby, that is totally different, because you are holding the baby and usually you are rocking slowly.

Changing your baby's diaper is unavoidable at some point, even if it's stimulating for your baby. Stay tuned, and I will explain more in the next chapter about diaper changing.

Bathing is also very stimulating for a baby, especially newborns to four-month-olds. It is best to wait to bathe your baby until it is turning dark outside. That is because darkness creates a release of melatonin in your baby's brain to help your baby relax and be able to sleep through the night. Rays of light, however, diminish melatonin levels. Therefore, you will want to bathe your baby in a low-lit room as it is getting dark outside. Doing this will enable your baby to better handle the stimulation of a bath.

Some babies, newborns especially, will cry throughout their entire bath due to all the stimulation. If you give the baths in the early morning, usually you will have an overstimulated baby the entire day, and by evening, you will probably both be crying! Bathing a baby in a softly lit room after dark can help them recover from overstimulation.

To make bath time less overwhelming for your baby, try breast-feeding on only one side first. Next, bathe your baby, apply lotion or do a coconut oil rub down if you wish, which I will explain later. Next, put on her diaper and clothes, etc. Then breastfeed on the other side. Feeding the baby on one side only before the bath helps her feel comfortably satiated during the bath, even if she is not completely full.

You can also swaddle your baby loosely with a towel to give her a bath. This can help your baby stay calm. Swaddling your infant just long enough to lower her in the water and pour water over her body pre-bath might make that she cries less for the rest of the bath. When you are ready to apply soap, you could slowly open the swaddle on one side and bathe your baby on that side, then close it again and repeat on the other side.

Once it is dark outside, a mother's breastmilk contains melatonin to enable her baby to relax and sleep through the night. So if you save some breastfeeding until after the bath, it will help her relax, and then you can put her to bed in a much more relaxed state. Even if you are bottlefeeding, I would recommend this method, because feeding a baby after bathing seems to help her relax.

Also, be aware, a newborn baby does not need a lot of bathing. They have a covering on their skin called vernix to protect their skin, and bathing them will remove that. Once you remove the vernix from your baby's skin, they become more prone to getting rashes and other skin irritations. Your newborn baby really does not need more than one or two baths a week. Of course, that would depend on your climate or temperature, and if your baby is sweating a lot, etc. If the baby is warm and sweating a lot, the first place that will become irritated are where there are rolls of fat, like under their armpits, creases of the legs, etc.

There is an amazing product called diaper rash cream you can apply to your baby's fat creases to eliminate irritation and redness. I apply it to my baby after every bath or whenever it's needed. I usually apply this in places like the underarms, creases in my baby's legs, and inside his elbows. Of course, this will depend on how fat your baby is. My babies were always quite fat, so they had big folds of fat and were susceptible to a lot of chafing in those areas. This cream is remarkable for its ability to remain on the skin for several days and is resistant to water or moisture. This eliminates redness and chafing. It also includes essential oils to kill bacteria. This product also works well for adults. It is common to get chafing and irritation of the skin, especially during the summer when it is warm, and you are sweating. I have learned to stock up on it when it is warm outside. Scan the QR code below with your camera if you would like to buy the diaper rash cream.

Doterra Diaper Rash Cream

This code contains an affiliate link. If you make a purchase through this link, I will receive a commission.

If you don't want to purchase this cream online, you will need to find a dealer in your area.

You can find body cloths that are antibacterial, and you don't need to use any soap with them. The cloth that I use contains silver to kill bacteria. I prefer using these for my baby when I need to clean their creases. The body cloths are especially helpful for the first couple of weeks because you don't want to submerge your baby in water until the cord has healed. I will wet the cloth using warm water. Using cool or cold water will be especially startling for the baby. Then, I simply give them a simple wash down with the cloth, being careful to get in any creases where they might get sweaty and chafed. Scan the code below to purchase the cloths.

Norwex Antibacterial body Cloths

This code contains an affiliate link. If you make a purchase through this link, I will receive a commission.

If you don't want to purchase these cloths online, you will need to find a dealer in your area.

If you really want your baby to smell lovely, a simple rubdown of lotion makes your baby smell amazing!

If you use an antibacterial body cloth for your baby, or apply lotion, it will stimulate your baby, so you will want to use the same guidelines I outlined for a bath.

Changing a baby's clothes is stimulating. Therefore, I only change my baby's clothes when I feel it is necessary, especially during those first couple of months. I follow the same guidelines as for a bath, if possible.

Burping is another one of those inevitable things—it has to be done. You don't want to pat your baby on the back; patting jolts your baby and is very stimulating. Instead, rub the baby's back in an upward motion while laying the baby across your shoulder; you can also alternate different positions–whatever works for your baby. Just be sure to rub and not pat. Patting can also exacerbate spit-up and make things like acid reflux worse.

I found it helpful to only nurse on one side, then burp the baby, then nurse on the other side and burp again. That seems to cut down on those annoying hiccups that can happen if a burp sits too long in their tummies. This is especially true in the first couple of months. However, after the baby is a little older, and doesn't get hiccups as easily anymore, you can wait to burp the baby until she has completed her feeding.

I found a way to check if a baby still has burps in her tummy. Since a baby's stomach is on her left side, I place her on my left leg facing inward. Then, I put my left hand around her waist, under her armpit. This allows me to feel if there are still burps in her stomach. It will feel like a bubble inside when she inhales deeply.

If possible, keep your baby away from loud noises. This can be any-thing from children screaming to loud music. When I am feeding the baby and my girls are around, they may not make any loud noises like screaming, yelling, or banging doors.

I recommend keeping your baby's bedroom as quiet as possible during nap times. A white noise machine will be your best friend to drown out noise. But even with white noise, it will be helpful for you to keep the noise down outside their bedroom. I try to use the most soundproof room in the house for the baby's bedroom.

Going to unfamiliar places and meeting unfamiliar people is often unavoidable. While it can be a source of overstimulation for some babies, it will not bother other babies. If I see my baby becoming overstimulated, I will try to leave at the earliest convenience for the baby. This can be a really tough one, so just do whatever works for you.

I try to eliminate a lot of extensive vacations, camp outs, etc. while my baby is still very young. At this age, babies are still easily overstimulated. Therefore, it's less stressful if you wait until they are six months old or older. By then, they can handle more excitement.

This list is not exhaustive because every baby is different, so there might be things that are stimulating for your baby that are not mentioned. Maybe your phone ringing, etc., even if it is fairly quiet, might startle and overstimulate your baby. Anything that startles them is overstimulating. Your baby's response will show you if there was an excessive amount of stimulation. If they look startled or jerk their head, hands, etc., it was probably overstimulating.

Being overtired is the second potential cause of your baby's fussiness. The next chapter explores that topic.

# CHAPTER 4

# Defining An Overtired Baby

OVERSTIMULATION AND OVER-TIREDNESS IN babies often go together. Keep this in mind: all your baby wants to do for the first four months is sleep. However, parents feel they have waited so long to actually see the baby that now it is time to engage with them. This results in an overwhelmed, overtired baby.

The problem is they don't know when to stop. Why put a baby to sleep when he is still happy and content? However, an environment that promotes relaxation is important for newborn to four-month-old babies to avoid becoming overtired. Many parents are not familiar with the cues that babies show when they are overtired. Several signs of over-tiredness are yawning, crying, or eyes darting back and forth. If you speak to them, they may refuse eye contact and look away. They may seem tense or clench their fists. In whatever way your baby expresses over-tiredness, they will seem frazzled, overwhelmed, or aloof.

In addition, many parents wait to put their babies to sleep until he already show signs of over-tiredness. If your baby is newborn to four months old, it is already too late; your baby is so overtired that you will have a hard time getting him to relax. The more overtired your baby is, the harder it is for him to fall asleep.

This pattern continues repeatedly throughout the day, and by evening, your baby is so excessively tired that she will be inconsolable and therefore, unable to sleep. That is why it is crucial to have your baby asleep before you see these telltale signs of over-tiredness.

It is also important to understand that an overtired or overstimulated baby will not sleep well. You may have heard the term that you should let your baby play longer so she sleeps better. While this has a balance–not giving your baby enough stimulation at wake times will make her take cat naps because she is under–tired and under-stimulated. However, too much stimulation and your baby will not sleep well either. The reason is that over-tiredness triggers the release of stress hormones in their brains. These two stress hormones, cortisol and adrenaline, keep the baby awake when she is tired and needs to sleep. Then, your baby has a hard time relaxing and sleeping soundly. Therefore, I have found it is better to put your baby to bed sooner rather than later. The same is true for adults. I think we as moms can all relate to sometimes feeling so tired that we can't sleep for a long time. However, when you finally fall sleep; you don't sleep well. That is because if our body is in a stressed mode from being overtired, we cannot sleep well either.

I do not believe in the term 'fighting sleep' for a baby. I believe the baby is overtired and overstimulated and trying so hard to fall asleep. It seems like they are angry and frustrated that they *have* to sleep. In reality, the stress hormones are raging, making that they *can't* sleep.

It's best to go only by your baby's cues to monitor how much stimulation they can take and how long their wake time should be. I learned not to worry about guidelines online that stated how much wake time my baby should have for their specific age.

I tried following the instructions I saw online or in a book for my baby's wake times. This resulted in an overstimulated and over-tired baby. Then she couldn't sleep, and there was lots of crying. As your baby gets older, she may have more playtime. However, only change playtime based on your child's cues, not on what someone suggests.

To recap the last 3 chapters, too much stimulation makes an over-tired baby. Then, because the baby is overtired, stress hormones are released in your baby's brain. Now your baby has a hard time relaxing. As a result, your baby will not fall asleep easily. Often the baby will cry excessively to release the tension inside, created by the stress hormones. When the baby finally falls asleep, she doesn't sleep well because she was excessively tired before falling asleep. Then the baby only takes catnaps or wakes up still upset and overtired. This cycle continues throughout the day, leading to an exhausted baby (and mom!) The model below is a good example of this.

The
Overstimulation
Cycle

- Baby gets overstimulated
- Overtiredness follows
- Stress hormones are released
- Excessive crying, difficulty falling asleep
- Doesn't sleep well, catnaps
- Wakes up, still upset, overtired

# CHAPTER 5

# The Importance of Routine and Habit

IT IS IMPORTANT TO create a routine as soon as possible after the baby is born. Finding a routine and sticking to it helps create security for a baby. Following a routine also helps your baby form habits. Some say that once a parent has shown a baby the same routine for three consecutive times, babies will take it as a habit.

Here is an example of a routine that I like to use: your baby wakes up from her nap, so you engage with her while changing her diaper. Engaging with her includes things like talking to her and singing to her. Next, you feed her, burp her and then put her back in her crib to sleep, and the cycle begins again.

I like this specific routine because it includes stimulating activities like diaper changing and interacting with the baby first when they wake up. It's best to engage with your baby right after they wake up if they're under four months. Even then, you don't want to overdo it.

If you breastfeed, you have an advantage, because breastmilk contains hormones to relax the baby. That's why I recommend putting the baby to sleep right after feeding and burping. In addition, the calming hormones in breast milk help compensate for the stimulation of changing your baby's diaper. In fact, you may have better success with this sleep plan if you are breastfeeding. However, if

I were giving the baby formula, I would still recommend following the same routine.

And just as an extra tip, you may wonder whether pumping has the same benefits as breastfeeding. Breastfeeding is still the best way to feed a baby, and here's why. A mother needs physical contact with her baby to provide maximum immunity for the baby. When a baby breast-feeds, the interaction between their saliva and the breast milk sends messages to the mother's brain. These messages convey to the mom's brain what nutrients the baby requires. This feedback allows the mother's body to supply the specific nutrients that the baby needs. Breast milk composition also adjusts for premature babies and changes throughout the day and during feedings. Strictly pumping or using donor milk disrupts the feedback loop between the mother and baby. Then, because of the lack of physical contact between the mother and baby during breastfeeding, the baby will have fewer immune system benefits. This is also why it is very important to only breastfeed when your baby is sick. The physical contact will allow the mother's body to provide specific nutrients that the baby is lacking when the baby's immunity is low.

You may question things like what if the routine gets interrupted? For example, your baby wakes up, and you change her diaper. Then, as she is eating, she makes a poopy mess; or she makes a mess after she is done eating, and you are ready to put her to bed. Obviously, you will still have to change the diaper again before placing the baby in her crib. You might also need to change her clothes. Keep reading and I will elaborate more on how to help the baby relax after stimulation in order to sleep if something like this should happen.

Burping, of course, is necessary after breastfeeding. However, if you rub your baby's back gently, like I suggested, it will not be nearly as stimulating. In fact, it might help your baby relax and fall asleep better.

It just makes sense to feed your baby and then burp before bed because your baby will have a full tummy and be relaxed from the breast milk. And then, because your baby is relaxed from her feeding and ready to sleep, it also makes sense to place her in her crib for nap time.

I prefer to put my baby on her tummy so she can move around and get comfortable, and most babies prefer their tummies. Also, if there is still a burp trapped in her tummy, she will probably be able to squirm a little and the burp will come to the surface. If you put her on her back, it might be harder for her to fall asleep. This is also a good way for your baby to get tummy time. However, do what works for you and your baby.

You might wonder, will my baby cry if I put her to bed after feeding without rocking her to sleep first? The answer is—usually not if your baby is in a relaxed state. My baby had no trouble falling asleep because I created a calm atmosphere. Since I fed her and the breastmilk relaxed her, it was easier for her to fall asleep in her crib. If you have created a calm atmosphere with little to no stimulation just before bedtime, and the baby is not overtired, it is much easier for her to fall asleep independently.

Talking a lot to the baby just before bedtime and delaying her bedtime can make her unable to sleep by herself.

Often the reason a baby cries when you put her in her crib is because she is overtired and overstimulated. In fact, your baby wants to sleep! If you make it easy for your baby to fall asleep, you will have a more relaxed baby that doesn't mind bedtime.

There is an exception to this. A newborn baby might want more cuddles the first few days after birth, and that is okay. Just be sure not to overstimulate her and put her to bed as soon as she is ready to sleep or is already asleep. That way, she learns to associate her bed with sleep.

Also, some babies have evening fussing spells, and babies under four months sometimes need lots of cuddles in the evening to help them stay calm. I will explain more about this later.

If your baby has a hard time falling asleep in the crib, I recommend adding more saturated fat and/or DHA into your baby's diet. These fats are crucial in helping your baby relax. The best way to do that if you are breastfeeding is by incorporating more of these essential fats into your diet. As a result, these fats will pass through your milk to your baby, helping the baby fall asleep easier. If you are bottlefeeding, you can add these fats to your baby's bottle to aid sleep. I explain this more in Chapter 6 about how to include these fats in your diet.

In addition, if a mom is stressed during breastfeeding, she will pass the stress hormone, cortisol, onto her baby through her milk. High cortisol makes it difficult for your infant to fall asleep and sleep well. I recommend a mom doing deep breathing while breast-feeding to lower her cortisol levels. Here, you will inhale through your nose and hold your breath as long as you can. Then open your mouth and exhale slowly. Another way to lower cortisol is to listen to cortisol-reducing sounds. You can find several sounds that lower cortisol on YouTube by typing in "cortisol-lowering sounds" in the search bar. Ideally, you would use headphones to listen. Also, one of the best ways I have found to reduce cortisol is by walking. Taking a couple of minutes to walk around your house before breastfeeding could make a difference. In addition, being outside helps lower cortisol as well.

If the baby still has a problem falling asleep independently, here are some recommendations. First, it is essential that your baby be totally relaxed before you place her in her crib. Take some time to evaluate your baby before placing her in her crib. Are her eyes wide awake and alert? If your baby is wide awake after the feeding or not in a relaxed state as you are ready to put her in bed, here are some tips to try. You could rock her to get her relaxed. When she seems relaxed and ready to sleep, now you could place her in her crib to sleep. Another way to get your infant into a relaxed state pre-nap is through touch and massage. Rubbing your baby's hair in upward strokes can be relaxing for your baby. There's a method that works amazingly for some babies to relax, and that is by taking your finger and, in a downward motion, rubbing softly from the center of their forehead down to their nose. Then alternate between that and stroking their eyebrows from inward to outward. You will need to try several things to see what works well to relax your baby well before her nap.

You can also put her in her crib and then use what I call the "distract to relax" method to help her relax and fall asleep. Here, you will do two things simultaneously to distract your baby. The reason this seems to work well is that a baby cannot focus on more than two things at once. If you distract them with two things; they cannot focus on crying. Some forms of distraction might include rubbing your baby's hair, singing softly to your baby, or patting her bottom gently. If you do two of those simultaneously, your baby cannot focus on crying, and this will help the baby relax and fall asleep. Two forms of distraction that I have found to work well together are singing "sh," "sh," "sh," over and over softly, while patting my baby's bottom gently. However, do what works for you and your baby. Here again, you could try the face massage I mentioned above. Then, just as baby is drifting off to sleep, stop rubbing your baby, singing to your baby, rubbing baby's face, etc. and see if she can continue falling asleep by herself. (I suggest just stopping all soothing without moving or leaving the room, because that can startle baby awake again.) In this way, a baby is so relaxed, it is easy for your baby to continue falling asleep by herself. I would continue this strategy and see if you can use relaxing techniques less and less so baby self-settles more each time. This can teach your baby to fall asleep independently. If, however, your baby needs constant soothing in order to fully fall asleep, that's okay. It's more important to keep a baby relaxed, even if that means constant soothing until he or she is fully asleep.

You can also rock your baby to relax her just before bed, then place her in her crib to sleep. Then if she still struggles to sleep, you could use the distract to relax method once she's in her crib.

I prefer a baby falling asleep independently after you placed her in her bed. The more relaxed your baby is before you place her in her crib, the easier it will be for your baby to do so. However, if your infant needs extra assistance to fall asleep, that's okay. I prefer not to let a newborn baby cry a lot until she falls asleep. The point is to create a restful, happy vibe around naptime. If your baby has to cry herself to sleep all the time, especially as a newborn, your baby learns to associate bedtime with crying. We want to prevent this at this tender age. (Later, when your baby is older, and can handle more stimulation, they may cry a little as they are settling down for sleep. More about that later.)

The reason I prefer to teach my baby the habit of falling asleep in her crib is that it is so much easier in the long run. It is much harder to rock your baby to sleep and try to transfer her into her crib without waking her up. Then, if she wakes up, you have to start the entire process again. It may take some time, but if you follow this routine every day, your baby will form a habit of falling asleep once you place her in her crib.

If you always rock your baby to sleep, it will become a habit for your baby to rely on your rocking her to enable her to fall asleep. At some point in your child's life, you will want to teach her to sleep with no need to be rocked. I found it is easier to teach my baby proper sleep habits from the beginning, rather than needing to break bad habits later. Again, it also makes a baby more secure because of the consistency/security connection.

I have also found that implementing a routine and helping my baby form habits helps them sleep through the night easier and sooner. Most babies should be able to sleep through the night by 3 to 6 months old. Of course, this will depend on your baby. Babies that are bigger at birth can usually sleep through the night sooner than smaller babies. One of my babies was 10 pounds at birth, and she was sleeping eight hours at night at six weeks old. However, if you had a preemie, it could go longer, since they do not weigh as much as they would have if they had been born full-term.

Getting your baby to fall asleep in the crib during the day will teach your baby to do the same at night. Then, if something random wakes her during the night, it is much easier for her to go back to sleep with no intervention from you.

If you always rock your baby to sleep during the day, she's going to require the same if she wakes up at night. It is normal for a baby to wake up multiple times a night. However, a baby should be able to fall asleep readily again. However, if they have been taught the habit of only falling asleep in your arms, they will require the same at night. That is why rocking your baby to sleep during the day can be detrimental to getting her to sleep well at night.

Of course, if you are more comfortable holding your baby until she falls asleep, that is fine. Do whatever you are most comfortable with and what works for you and your baby.

I have learned that it is also best to put your baby to sleep in only one specific place. Usually, this is the crib. The problem is, if you place your baby in a crib one day and in a bassinet the next, it will be confusing for your baby. Or if you put your baby in a bassinet during the day and a crib during the night, it might be confusing as well. That's why it's ideal to stick with one location for your baby to sleep. That way, your baby associates only one specific place with sleeping. I recommend putting your baby to sleep where you want her to sleep for the next one to two years. If you put them to sleep in a bassinet now, before too long, you will have to switch to a crib. This can be unsettling for a young baby. The reason it's important to have a specific place for your baby to sleep is because of what I called the familiarity–security connection. Let me explain.

Let's say your baby is four months old, and you get invited to a family gathering. At this family gathering, most of the people are unfamiliar to your baby. Therefore, your baby may prefer to have only Mom hold her in this situation. The reason is that Mom is the most familiar person to her at this point. Your baby does not recognize anybody else in the room but Mom. Thus, your baby feels most secure being with her mom.

Obviously, the reason for this is that Mom has taken care of her baby every day. She has fed her baby when she was hungry, comforted her when she cried, and nurtured her baby in many other ways. Mom has proved to her baby that she can trust Mom to take care of her.

As a result, Mom is the most familiar and trusted person to her baby. Thus, the baby feels most secure being with her mom.

In the same sense, a baby learns to trust something familiar, like her own bed, blanket, etc. Hence, familiarity brings security to a baby. This is why putting your baby in the same bed every time brings security.

You may question why I mentioned nothing about swaddling. For my first baby, I swaddled her as a newborn. The problem was, after a couple of weeks, it was time to remove the swaddle. This was confusing for her, because she had been in the habit of only falling asleep with her swaddle on. For that reason, I prefer not to swaddle. I feel it is best to only implement routines and habits that you can sustain for the first four to 6 months, if possible. This creates security for your baby.

Another thing to consider is if your baby is in a relaxed state and you are ready to put her to bed, swaddling may stimulate her. Then it will be more difficult for your baby to relax again and, ultimately, fall asleep. However, do what works best for you and your baby. Of course, if you decide to swaddle, your baby would need to sleep on her back only.

Something to consider about swaddling, this inhibits a baby's Moro or startle reflex. This can lead to retained reflexes later and affect a baby negatively. It also inhibits movement, and the less a baby can move freely, the less their brain can grow. Heather

Mrak talks about how she started working with children who were behind in development and she learned how much inhibited movement as a baby contributed to this problem. She is an expert in infant brain development and can be found on Instagram @babysbestbrain.

With that said, it can be comforting for a newborn baby to be swaddled for the first couple of hours/days after birth. That is because swaddling makes a newborn feel like they did in the womb. So again, do what you are comfortable with, and works for you and your baby.

If your newborn needs extra comfort, skin to skin can make a difference. Here, you will remove all your clothing from your stomach to your chest. Then, you will remove all your baby's clothing except her diaper. Then the baby lies across your chest. Your body temperature will warm the baby, and it feels very comforting to your baby to feel your body heat and skin.

Some moms may want to co-sleep with their babies. However, I only recommend this if your baby is a newborn. For the first couple of days after birth, a baby may be unsettled and need extra comfort. Providing skin to skin, as mentioned before, can provide security for your baby. However, I don't recommend making this a daily practice. Again, one day you will have to put your baby in her crib, and then it will be hard to do so because she has formed a habit of only sleeping with you. However, do whatever you are comfortable with and works best for you.

A home birth can be less stimulating for a baby, and a routine can be implemented right after birth. However, you should give birth wherever you feel most comfortable. (I have written a book called *How to Have a Faster, Less Painful Natural Birth*. In this book, I share my experience of going from intensely painful 18-24 hour births to a fast, less painful 3-hour birth. More details at the back of this book.)

Sometimes a baby seems to want interaction when he or she is breastfeeding or taking a bottle. Here, maintaining eye contact is a great way to bond with your baby without overstimulating her. Stroking your baby's hair is relaxing for a baby and can be a great way to bond and engage with your baby without causing overstimulation.

So, by now, you've gotten the point that a baby just has a certain amount of energy and attention span. If you overdo it, that's where you get a crying, overstimulated, overtired baby. Then, the more overstimulated and overtired your baby gets, the harder it is for her to fall asleep. As the baby gets older, she will want more engagement and look away for a bit but look back at you again and again for more. It will be very tempting to talk and engage a little too much with your baby after she wakes up, especially if she keeps looking back at you for more engagement. But even if they look back time after time, keep in mind you still have the diaper to change and the baby to feed. If you stimulate too much too soon, you will have an overwhelmed, overtired, crying baby by the time you are done and ready to put her to bed.

It is helpful to stay at home more in order to maintain a routine and good sleep habits, especially in the first couple of months. This holds true if you have a baby who is overstimulated by unfamiliar places and people. It's so much harder to stick to a routine when you are at someone else's house. However, you don't want to be a hermit either, so do what works best for you.

Even if your baby is used to falling asleep in her crib at home, that doesn't mean she will do the same at someone else's house. Sometimes my babies will, and sometimes they won't. Babies are used to sleeping in their own beds and can feel uneasy when sleeping somewhere new, which can make it difficult for them to fall asleep. Not only are their surroundings different, but it feels different. In that case, I will place the baby in the crib, but if my baby just cries, I will often rock my baby to sleep.

You might give your baby a small, cuddly blanket or comfort item to keep them company in their crib around 3-4 months old. Usually by this time, your baby can move around more in the crib. If your baby is lying on her tummy, there's less chance of her getting it over her mouth and suffocating. They love to cuddle with fuzzy, warm things as they fall asleep, and this makes falling asleep a pleasant experience.

I rarely use a pacifier because if your baby is in a relaxed atmosphere, he usually will not need it. Once you give a pacifier to your baby and put him in his crib, it will fall out over and over. This will not only disrupt your baby's sleep, but you will create a routine and a habit for him if you keep giving him his pacifier. This will create an overtired/overstimulated baby. It's ideal if he only falls asleep with some type of comfort item because it will not fall out like a pacifier.

Sometimes my baby would be fussier during the evening, and in those times, I have been glad for a pacifier. However, because my babies did not get in the habit of needing a pacifier, they rarely wanted to suck on it for very long. However, do whatever works for you and your baby.

As I have consulted with tongue tie and jaw development experts, I've learned a lot about the negative effects of pacifiers. Pacifiers will cause poor jaw development, leading to crowded teeth and airway issues later. This will majorly affect a child's sleep. A pacifier here and there is fine, but a pacifier at every nap will cause problems later. There are pacifiers that are better than others for proper oral development; Nini is a good brand. Philips Advent Soothie, Dr. Brown's happy paci, Jollypop pacifier, Lilli and Me pacifier are all second choice. The bulbous ones or orthodontist ones are the worst and look nothing like a mother's breast. However, keep in mind that all pacifiers can cause poor oral development when a baby sucks on them often.

You will want to continue this routine or whatever routine works for you, from the age of newborn on. Then, as your baby grows older, she will tolerate more stimulation and play. But only allow as much interaction as your baby can handle without overstimulating her. If your baby cries when you put her to bed, she has probably been overstimulated a little. But because she has learned to fall asleep in her crib, she might cry for a couple of minutes, but it will not be excessive. In fact, if you have given your baby a comfort item, like I mentioned above, they will usually grab their "cuddly" and easily fall asleep. You have reinforced the idea that falling asleep is pleasant because babies love snuggly comfort items as they fall asleep. Also, all the times you put your baby to bed before she became overtired contributed to the idea that sleeping is a positive experience. Remember, babies love to sleep.

As your baby grows older, the benefits of implementing a routine besides getting them to fall asleep in their crib become more evident. Creating a routine early on makes things easier as they grow up. They learn to expect it and feel secure. Since I created an environment of relaxation, comfort, and security for my babies as they fell asleep, they hardly ever cried when they woke from a nap. If they did, it was usually because something startling or loud woke them. It was very common, especially once they were a couple of months old, for my babies to wake up and start cooing. Another contributing factor was the assurance they felt from falling asleep in their crib every time and knowing exactly how they got there.

If you rock your baby to sleep and then place her in her crib, she will not know how or when you placed her there. When she wakes up, it can be startling to be in different surroundings than she was when she fell asleep, and she starts crying. An example of this would be, let's say, you go on a trip and stay at a hotel to sleep for the night. The next morning you wake up and momentarily you think, "Where Am I?" Obviously, the reason you wonder at first is that your surroundings are different than normal. Then, of course, you recall taking a trip and coming to the hotel. However, if you fall asleep in your own bed, you never wake up in the morning and wonder where you are. That's because you wake up every morning in the same surroundings. This is also true for your baby and is another example of the familiarity–security connection.

Of course, if you prefer to always rock your baby to sleep and then place her in her crib, that's fine too. Whatever works for you and your baby.

# CHAPTER 6
# Troubleshooting

THERE WILL BE TIMES when, despite your best efforts not to overstimulate your baby, it will happen. Maybe your phone rings just before you place the baby in bed, and it startles her. If my baby seems really startled and overstimulated while I am still holding her, I will try to rock her a little to calm her and get her into a relaxed state before putting her in her crib. If she still cries after she is put in bed, I can let her fuss for a few minutes, and see if she calms down.

If a newborn is not too overstimulated, they usually cry for a few minutes, and then they quickly doze off. However, if they are really overstimulated, excessive crying only intensifies their overstimulation. In that case, I would try some tips I outlined earlier, especially the "distract to relax" strategy.

### Solutions For Diaper Rash

If your baby has a diaper rash, it can cause pain. This will make it harder for your baby to sleep well. As soon as your baby urinates even a little, it will hurt their bottom. Two products that I have found to work the best are dōTERRA brand, diaper rash cream and Redmond bentonite clay. If the rash is mild, just the cream, or the clay sprinkled on, should work fine. (An empty spice shaker with sizable holes can serve as a container for the clay. This will allow you to shake the clay evenly onto your baby's bottom.) However, if the rash is more severe, I will first apply the diaper rash cream and then sprinkle the Redmond clay on top. Applying both creates a thick barrier between your baby's bottom and the urine. This allows the baby's reddened skin to heal quicker. As mentioned before, the diaper rash cream is resistant to moisture, and is amazing for this purpose. You can purchase the clay from Nature's Warehouse by scanning the QR code below. If you don't have internet access, you can purchase it from New Light Health at 717-692-3500. For the diaper rash cream, you would need to find a DoTerra dealer in your area. Or you can scan the QR code below to purchase the diaper rash cream.

**Redmond clay powder**

**Doterra Diaper Rash Cream**

This code contains an affiliate link. If you make a purchase through this link, I will receive a commission.

If you don't have the diaper rash cream on hand, you can also apply coconut oil or a gentle, herbal salve to your baby's bottom. Then sprinkle Redmond clay on top. This can work well too for a moderate-to-severe rash.

If you want an inexpensive, nontoxic source of baby powder for daily use to prevent diaper rash, I recommend non-gmo corn-starch. If you want it to have a lovely scent, you can add a couple of drops of lavender and/or chamomile essential oil. Then mix it to distribute the oils evenly throughout the cornstarch. I recommend using a shaker with sizable holes for easy application. You can also buy nontoxic baby powder at various health food stores.

Something to consider if your baby has diaper rash a lot, there can be some root causes behind it. One is antibiotic use. If you had a C-section, you were positively given antibiotics. Antibiotics wreak havoc on a mom's gut. If mom is breastfeeding, this gut issue passes to baby and can cause diaper rash and tummy distress for baby. Keep reading and I will cover this more later under the headline *Remedies for Your Infant's /Tummy Troubles.*

## What to Do If Your Baby Makes a Big Poopy Mess Just Before or After You Put Her to Bed

So, back to the question: what if I am feeding her and she poops in her diaper after I have already changed it? Obviously, her diaper will have to be changed again. In that case, I recommend feeding the baby until she is satisfied enough that she will not cry, but still not completely satiated. You want to save some feeding for after the diaper change. Then, I would change her diaper and come back again to finish feeding. That way, you will still feed her again, and that might help her relax in order to fall asleep more easily. If it's hard for her to relax and sleep after the diaper change because it was stimulating too close to bedtime, you can try to rock her to calm her down a little and help her relax. Then you can put her in her crib, and if she is still overstimulated, you can try the "distract to relax" strategy.

But what if she poops in her diaper after you have already changed and fed her? Of course, you will need to change her diaper again and possibly her clothes before placing her into bed. Now, there is going to be a bit of a problem because it will stimulate the baby just before you place her in bed. This is if you are using the routine in the order that I have explained. Again, I suggest trying the strategies that I listed above and finding something that works to relax her so she can fall asleep in her bed.

## Remedies for Your Infant's Gas/Tummy Troubles

If your baby has a hard time falling asleep, or staying asleep, it is very common for a baby to have tummy troubles. If you are breast-feeding, sometimes a baby will react to things you are eating. One common problem can be dairy. You could eliminate that from your diet and see if that helps.

If you are breastfeeding, sometimes if you eat spicy foods, it can give your baby a tummy ache. I discovered that if I fill an empty gelatin capsule with either baking soda or cream of tartar, and take that along with my spicy meal, my baby does not react to spicy things I ate.

If you are feeding formula, sometimes you might have to switch to another kind because it can cause a fussy baby. Alternatively, you might have to switch to goat's milk formula, which is easier on a baby's tummy.

There are also many tinctures out there to try for tummy distress. One thing I have found helpful when my baby has any kind of tummy distress is to open a capsule of a good enzyme and mix it with some milk kefir. Then, using an oral syringe, I slowly drop the kefir into the baby's mouth. I have found it works best if I give my baby the kefir and enzyme mixture before a feeding. Often, I would forget until after I was done nursing, and I could still tell a difference. For the first couple of months, I did this for almost every feeding because it really helped get those burps up and reduced tummy troubles.

If you are breastfeeding, you can also drink the kefir to add more probiotics to your gut or take some enzymes when you eat and see if that makes a difference for your baby.

You can make your own kefir at home. Kefir is made with raw cow's or goat's milk and kefir grains. The grains look like small white balls, and they are the starter of the kefir. You simply add about 1 tablespoon of kefir grains to 1 quart of milk. I use A2, grass-fed, raw cow's milk. Then let that sit on your counter until it becomes thick, almost like yogurt. (Do not use a metal container when you are fermenting your kefir. This will inhibit the fermentation process.) This might take anywhere from 12 to 24 hours, depending on how warm the room is. If you want it done faster, you can place it in a warm spot. However, be sure to keep it away from your oven as intense heat will kill the grains. Next, you strain the kefir grains from the milk, and mix the kefir to make it nice and smooth.

This process changes the structure of the milk. The kefir grains will ferment the milk, and the grains will feed off of the lactose in the milk and turn it into a probiotic-rich drink instead. Once the milk with the kefir grains has become thick, the kefir grains have eaten most of the lactose. Individuals who have lactose intolerance might be able to tolerate kefir, because there is very little lactose in kefir. Kefir also contains enzymes to aid in the digestion of lactose. The fermentation process will also increase the nutritional content of the milk.

Like us, kefir grains need food to stay alive. Their food source is lactose in milk. Once they have eaten all the lactose in milk, they will die. For that reason, once you have made a batch of kefir, you will want to strain the kefir grains and place them in fresh milk, and place that jar in the fridge. If you refrigerate the grains, they will consume the lactose at a much slower rate. To make kefir again, strain the kefir grains from the refrigerated milk, add fresh milk, and place it in a warm spot to ferment. Then you can begin the cycle again.

The leftover strained milk is not truly kefir. It will also be thin. You can either dump it or let it sit at room temperature. It will thicken like kefir, even without the grains. I would always let mine sit at room temperature. Then after it thickened, I would give it to my girls to drink like kefir. My girls loved kefir so much, they would drink this right up and not even realize it wasn't truly kefir. It tastes similar.

When storing kefir grains in the fridge for a long time, make sure to add sufficient milk for their food. Too little milk equals not enough lactose for the kefir grains. Then they will die. For example, if I leave my kefir grains in the fridge for one week, I will add 3 to 4 cups of milk to 1 tablespoon of kefir grains. For two weeks of storage in the fridge, I will double the amount of milk.

You might also want to make another batch of kefir right after the first one. In that case, strain the kefir grains from the first batch and add them to a new jar with fresh milk to make another batch.

You can use your kefir grains repeatedly and indefinitely. As long as they have a constant source of lactose and are not exposed to extreme heat, they remain healthy. The kefir grains will multiply. The more you make kefir, the more your kefir grains will increase in size and number.

Is it really safe to use raw milk to make kefir? You may be questioning. What about E. coli and other bacteria in the milk? According to studies that were done, kefir grains contain antibacterial properties that will kill E. coli, salmonella, and other bacteria if there are any present in the milk.

Kefir has a pleasant sour taste. The flavor takes some time to get used to. I added sweeteners like maple syrup and stevia to my baby's kefir at first to make it more appealing and less tart. Later, I will make it less sweet and just use stevia. Some stevia on the market has been laced with chemicals; organic will be your best option. You can also use other sweeteners. It's not recommended to sweeten kefir with honey. Honey's antibiotic effect may eradicate the beneficial probiotics found in kefir. In addition, you should never give honey to a baby under one because it can cause infant botulism.

You can buy kefir grains from the kefir lady. She can also help you get started and answer questions you may have. To contact the kefir lady or purchase kefir grains, you can call her at 517-610-8366, or you can use the code below on your camera to go to her website.

The Kefir Lady Website

You can buy kefir at grocery stores, especially the large chains. You can find it in the refrigerated dairy section, particularly with the yogurt. However, if you want the best results, homemade kefir is the way to go, especially for a baby who has tummy distress, because homemade kefir has significantly more probiotics than store-bought options. To give you an example, store-bought kefir contains around 10 strains of probiotics; homemade contains 40 to 60 strains. I would suggest that if you know someone who makes it at home with raw milk, to buy it from them instead of the pasteurized version at stores. I have found that store-bought, low-fat, pasteurized kefir seems to add to my baby's tummy distress. I suspect it's the pasteurization that causes it. For this reason, I can only recommend homemade kefir for this purpose.

You may wonder, won't milk kefir create digestive problems for my baby if I make kefir with cow's milk? My baby never had a problem with kefir. However, they became gassy and got diarrhea from straight cow's milk and even yogurt. Kefir was my arsenal for any stomach distress. I even used kefir for my newborn babies with no problems. However, since goats' milk is closer in structure to human mothers' milk, you can always use goat's milk instead if you feel more comfortable with that. Again, just be sure it is raw goat's milk, and not pasteurized goat's milk.

Since there is research that a premature baby cannot digest cow's milk, I would probably use goat's milk to make kefir for her. The kefir contains probiotics to help the baby digest the cow's milk. However, just to be safe, I would just use goat's milk.

You will want to be aware that there is also an option to buy water kefir. Water kefir is not the same as milk kefir and should not be used as such. You can buy it at grocery stores. It is usually near the refrigerated drinks, like kombucha. Water kefir can also be made at home using a base of water instead of milk. Water kefir grains are neutral/tan in color. Milk kefir grains are white.

I have also found that kefir works wonderfully to relieve the symptoms of teething for a baby. I will explain in Chapter 8 about those benefits.

You may also need to implement probiotics in your baby's diet. If you had a C-section, you were given antibiotics. Antibiotics wreak havoc on a mom and baby's gut. Antibiotics cause gut dysbiosis. Kefir is loaded with probiotics and may work well, but you may need to implement a probiotic besides kefir, or maybe it works best for you to simply give baby a probiotic supplement. I suggest both you and baby take some kind of probiotic, because if baby has gut dysbiosis, she probably got it from you. If you are breastfeeding, your gut health gets passed on to your baby, good or bad. For that reason, it makes sense to give probiotics not only to the baby, but to the mom as well. Below are some baby probiotics you could try.

**Baby Probiotics**

This code contains an affiliate link. If you buy a product with this link, I will get a commission.

**Love bug Toddler Probiotics**

The first probiotic brand above is called Optibac Probiotic Baby Drops-Vegan Probiotic for Newborn Babies. This company is located in the United Kingdom, so it will be difficult to call them if you live in the U.S. Therefore, if you have limited internet access to order this product, I suggest emailing them at: myorder@opti bacprobiotics.com. You can check to see if Target carries them. If they don't have them in store, they might be able to order them for you.

The next one listed is my personal favorite, called Lovebug Toddler Probiotics. This company is also in the United Kingdom, so I can only offer an email and an address for you. I once supplemented my baby with another mom's breast milk. Unknown to me, she had taken antibiotics at the time of pumping and forgot to tell me. My baby started getting diaper rash that would not quit. By the time I figured out what was wrong, my baby had eczema as well. She continued breaking out in eczema after that frequently. I tried these various lotions and creams, but the rash kept returning. Then I tried these, and the rash quickly cleared up and has not returned since. My baby was also happier when taking these probiotics daily. These are designed for toddlers, so if you want to use them for a younger baby, I would use less than the recommended dosage and mix it in breastmilk or formula rather than water. It has no taste, so it's easy for babies to take. You can contact them here if you don't have internet access: 115 East 34th Street, Suite 1506, New York, NY 10156, Customer Service Support: hello@lovebugprobiotics.com.

You may also consider dairy allergies if your baby has digestive distress, constant diaper rash, and foamy, green, or mucus-looking bowel movements. One breastfeeding mom has issues where her baby was waking every hour at night until 12:00 AM and at 2, 4, and 6 AM just to have a bowel movement. The first issue I uncovered was a tongue-tie. After that was resolved, the baby was still waking up to poop. Come to find out, it was a dairy allergy. After removing dairy from her diet, she emailed me to tell me baby had slept his first 8-hour stretch. Baby was 8 weeks old.

Another thing to consider is that your baby might have a tongue and/or lip tie, which can contribute to tummy distress. Chapters 9 to 14 will be about mouth ties and where to go if you suspect your baby has a tongue and/or lip tie.

Labor can cause problems in your baby's nervous and skeletal system. This can lead to tight muscles, and ultimately pain and discomfort in your baby. Then your baby will not feed well or sleep well. In my experience, a bodyworker or cranial therapist can do wonders to relieve tight muscles, especially in a baby. They work with the body's fascia, which is connective tissue just under the skin. A bodyworker or cranial therapist differs from a typical chiropractor. The method they use is very gentle and relieves pressure throughout your baby's body.

I also suggest checking out the L-Reuteri yogurt information at the bottom of this chapter.

And just for context, I am not a doctor, and this information is for educational purposes only. This information is not intended to diagnose, treat, cure, or prevent any disease. Consult with your doctor before changing your or your baby's diet.

**The Specific Nutrients Your Baby Needs to Sleep Well**

One reason your baby can have a difficult time falling asleep easily is a lack of saturated fat and/or DHA in a baby's diet. Saturated fat and DHA are essential for your baby's brain development. In addition, it helps your baby's brain to relax and fall asleep more easily. These crucial fats are like brain food for your infant. If you are breastfeeding, your breastmilk contains some fat and DHA. However, if your diet does not contain enough of these important nutrients, you cannot supply them to your baby. Cod liver oil is a significant source of DHA. For this reason, including some cod liver oil in your diet could make a difference.

Butter, cream, and coconut oil contain good relaxing fats called saturated fats. For the butter and cream, I would opt for grass-fed if possible. One thing I enjoy when I am breastfeeding is smothering a slice of healthy, whole-grain bread with butter and then toasting it. Then, I will even slather it with some more butter to melt into the toast. This is incredibly delicious. You could even top it with some cheese to melt into the toast as well. If you are breastfeeding, it will supply the fat in the butter to your baby through your milk. Kefir with extra cream and the L-Reuteri yogurt recipe at the bottom of this chapter would be helpful for getting more saturated fats in a breastfeeding mom's diet as well.

You can also rub your baby down with coconut oil, because that is also high in saturated fat. Extra virgin and virgin coconut oil will be your best bet because they contain more saturated fat. Extra-virgin contains the most. If I do this in the evening, it seems to work effectively to help the baby fall asleep easier the next day.

I will strip her down to her diaper and rub down her entire body with the coconut oil. Because her body will absorb it through her skin, it will have the same effect as if you would take it internally and it would come through your breast milk.

Doing the rubdown at dusk with low lighting or under red lights can help your baby handle the stimulation because of the higher levels of melatonin in your baby's brain in a dark room. Here again, leave some breastfeeding until after you are done rubbing her down and putting her clothes back on. That way, the breast milk will help your baby relax from the stimulation.

For a delightful smell, I would add a couple of drops of lavender oil to the coconut oil. That is optional, however. Also, because a baby's skin is relatively dry anyway, this works really well to keep the baby's skin moisturized.

The coconut oil rub down is great because if you are giving a bottle, you can still have a way of getting those saturated fats into your baby's system. Even if you are breastfeeding, it works wonderfully to add more fats in this way. During the first four months of breast feeding, I did this every day because I thought it helped my baby sleep better the following day.

There were times, however, that I would do the coconut oil rub downs during the day, and in that case, I would just strip her down to her onesie and her diaper. Then I would slather my hand with coconut oil, and slide my hand under her onesie, and rub her down that way. It's not nearly as stimulating if you don't need to take all her clothes off to do it and put them back on again. Just be sure you don't do this just before bedtime, especially if your baby is from newborn to four months old; the best time will be just after the baby wakes up and you are changing her diaper, anyway.

Magnesium is a relaxant. Therefore, magnesium supplements might be helpful too if you take them and they come through your breastmilk to your baby. Just be aware, too much magnesium can cause diarrhea, so you don't want to take too much at one time.

If you're not nursing, magnesium can't pass to your breastmilk by taking it internally. In that case, you can try topical magnesium and apply it to your baby. That will enable her to absorb it through her skin. In this case, Junior's Bedtime Lotion will work wonderfully. This product contains not only coconut oil, but magnesium as well. It also contains chamomile to aid your baby's relaxation. It also includes essential oils like lavender and makes your baby smell wonderful. The ingredients are all natural, and this product is available from 8 Sheep Organics. You can scan the code below to purchase. The code will give you $5 off your order.

**Junior's Bedtime Lotion**

This code contains an affiliate link. If you buy a product with this link, I will get a commission.

You can also email the company called 8 Sheep Organics your order at contact@8sheep.com to place an order. Just be sure to tell them you want to use the code BETH92074 because then you will get $5 off your order and I will get a commission as well. If you have no way to email them or use the link above, you can also get the same product from Botanique Bundles. You can call them at 424-248-7146.

## How to Eliminate Constipation in Your Baby, Especially as They Begin Eating.

It is common for babies to have constipation as they begin consuming food. This can become uncomfortable for them. Blackstrap molasses is helpful for this. If your baby is bottle-feeding, adding a tiny amount to their bottle each time should do the trick. In my experience, cracked cell chlorella is great for this as well. You can add a tiny amount to their bottle or add a little to their food. This is a superfood powder; it only takes a tiny amount for excellent results. Be sure you get only chlorella that has cracked cell. Unless they cracked the cell inside chlorella open to retrieve the nutrients, the chlorella itself is of little nutritional value. So, the container or bag the chlorella is in needs to say, "cracked cell." I would look for organic if possible. You can buy the molasses at Walmart or grocery stores. Chlorella is available at health food stores. Another option is the LoveBug Probiotics mentioned above, which are great for constipation.

And just for context, I am not a doctor, and this information is for educational purposes only. This information is not intended to diagnose, treat, cure, or prevent any disease. Consult with your doctor before making any changes to your or your baby's diet.

## What to Do If Your Baby Only Takes Catnaps

If your baby is taking cat naps, it's for a variety of reasons. If your baby is not overstimulated or overtired, I would check to see if your baby is getting enough to be well satiated. You need to be sure that your baby is getting enough milk at every feeding before you put her to bed. You want her to be satisfied. Then she will sleep longer and wake up and be hungry and ready to eat again. Then the cycle can continue. If your baby is not getting enough sleep, that will contribute to fussiness, and in order for your baby to sleep well, your baby needs to eat well.

Since I breastfed my babies, I am not an expert on how much milk your baby should be getting. There are a lot of resources online that will tell you.

If a baby is not getting enough milk at feedings, she will turn into a 'snacker.' A 'snacker' is not filling up enough, causing too frequent feedings and brief naps. A newborn should eat every 2 to 3 hours. Of course, as the baby gets older, she will go closer to 3 and occasionally 4 hours between feedings. Again, there are resources online to help you determine how long your baby can go between feedings for their specific age.

A mother's breast milk contains fore milk and hind milk. The fore milk comes first when the baby nurses and it is like sugar water. It does not sustain the baby for very long. Once the baby nurses and empties the breast of fore milk, the hind milk will follow. The hind milk is rich in fat and very satiating. Therefore, if you are not nursing long enough, the baby will never get the rich hind milk she needs to be satisfied.

However, babies will have growth spurts. During those times, they will want to eat more often for about three days before returning to their regular feeding schedule. Usually, the growth spurts are around 2-3 weeks, 6 weeks, 3 months, and 6 months. This might vary for different babies.

If your baby is 6 months old, he will be ready for baby food. Not giving your baby food when he is ready makes for a hungry baby who won't sleep well. I also recommend adding homemade kefir to your baby's diet because it is thicker in nature and more satiating than just milk. I explain more about kefir and how to implement it into your baby's diet in Chapter 8.

Cranial therapy might be helpful if your baby seems uncomfortable or has tight muscles.

Your baby might be under-stimulated or under-tired as well. Here, you could see if a longer wake window solves the problem. I would try implementing trace minerals or magnesium. If none of these seem to work, I would consider looking at the symptoms of a tongue, lip, or cheek tie. These mouth ties contribute majorly to your baby's inability to eat and/or sleep well. If your baby has a tongue, lip, or cheek tie, she will not be able to empty your breast and get to the hind milk. Thus, your baby will never be satiated and will take catnaps and need frequent feedings. I will explain more about tongue and lip ties in chapter 9 to 15.

**What to Do If Your Baby Wakes Up During the Night for No Reason**

If your baby is not sleeping well at night, my first question would be, are you rocking your baby to sleep during the day? If you are, I suggest you go back and read chapter 4. This chapter explains why rocking your baby to sleep during the day is detrimental to having him sleep well at night.

If you have implemented the strategies, I have outlined and your baby is still not sleeping through the night, it could be because of one of these causes. First, your baby might not be getting enough calories during the day to sustain him through the night. First, if you are breastfeeding, add more saturated fat to your diet; this makes your milk more satiating.

It's best to eliminate vegetable oils in your diet, like soy, canola, peanut, corn, and other vegetable oils, and replace them with saturated fats like coconut oil and grass fed, butter. Vegetable oils are devoid of nutrition and are toxic, whereas saturated fat is nutrient dense, and your baby desperately needs saturated fat to sleep longer stretches because it is more satiating. It's simple to swap saturated fats for vegetable oils. If a recipe calls for one of these oils, simply switch it out for butter or coconut oil, preferably extra virgin.

It is essential that your baby gets enough feeds during the day in order to sleep long stretches at night. In order for your baby to be able to sleep all night, I recommend feeding full feeds every 2-3 hours. If you are feeding every 3-1/2 to 4 hours, your baby is probably not getting enough calories to sleep 10 hours straight at night. Also, be aware that once you implement more nutrients, specifically fat, into your diet, your baby might want to sleep longer stretches during the day. That is because they are more satiated. However, just be careful your baby is not sleeping too long during the day and not getting enough feedings in or your baby will start waking up during the night to make up for it. I also recommend cluster feeding in the evening. This means feeding more often—sometimes every hour. This allows the baby to "tank up" to sustain the baby overnight so the baby can sleep longer.

You can also check how much milk your baby is consuming during the day. Then I would check resources online and see how much milk your baby needs at his specific age. Keep this in mind, however: if your milk contains more nutrients and fat, your infant will need less milk. We're talking about quality over quantity here. In addition, adding coconut oil, grass-fed butter and cream to your diet will boost the fat content in your milk as well and aid longer sleep at night.

As mentioned before, if your baby is 6 months old, he might be ready for food. Food is more satiating than milk and will sustain your baby longer than milk. Now, something very important to note, most moms will feed their babies traditional baby food which usually consists of baby food purees. However, there is one problem with this. Babies who eat only mainly pureed fruits and vegetables have poor jaw development, and the result is mouth breathing. This causes sleep problems, especially as they get older. I know this sounds weird; however; I learned this from Dr. Ben Miraglia. He has 30 years' experience resolving jaw development/sleep issues in children and the reason many of these children had sleep issues was because of only eating pureed foods as a baby. I will share the QR code for the link to this episode on Spotify below where he explains this. He is also on Instagram @drbenmiraglia and has many videos of his findings and shares his experience. In the last part of this book, you will learn more about jaw development and how it majorly affects your baby's sleep. In fact, jaw development will make or break your baby's sleep.

**Dr. Miraglia's podcast on poor jaw development/sleep issues from soft foods**

*He discusses soft foods and jaw development at 25:04 in the episode*

So you're probably wondering what to feed your baby then. I recommend baby-led weaning. This is when you give your baby foods that are easy to eat and let the baby feed herself. Obviously, you won't hand your six-month-old baby a piece of celery and expect them to eat it. You still need the food to be relatively soft at this age. One good option is baking sweet potatoes and then cutting them into strips about 2 inches long and about 4 inches wide. It's important that the food is long and fairly thick so the baby can grasp it and doesn't choke. If a baby can't pick it up, it's too small. You don't want to give babies round, slippery foods like grapes. You can cook apple slices and then let the baby feed herself. Cooked green beans are a great option. The reality is, six-month-old babies are much more able to eat foods, even some meat, when prepared properly to avoid choking. As baby grows older, you can add firmer foods and don't have to cook everything. This will help with optimal jaw development for your baby. I recommend Solid Starts to get started. They have a baby-led weaning cookbook, which I will link below. You can follow them on Instagram and have their own app, and they share so many tips to help you get started. It is important to wait until a baby shows interest in food before beginning this process, and they explain the signs to watch for that a baby is ready.

**Solid Starts Baby Led Weaning Cookbook**

**Another Baby Led Weaning Cookbook**

Something I have found to be helpful is adding kefir to your baby's diet around the age of 5 to 6 months. If you make the kefir from Jersey cow's milk, your baby will be more satiated and sleep longer during the night.

Jersey cow's milk contains more cream than other cow's milk. The extra fat from the cream translates to extra calories for your baby. When I switched from using Holstein cow's milk to Jersey milk, she fell asleep easier and slept more soundly both during the day and night because of the extra fat in Jersey milk.

Again, I am not a doctor, and this information is for educational purposes only. Consult with your doctor before making any changes to you or your baby's diet.

Another thing to consider is that your baby may have formed bad habits, like waking up during the night for a feeding. Obviously, if your baby is a newborn, night wakings are normal. However, unless your baby is a preemie, he should be able to sleep through the night by at least four to six months. If you feel like it's only out of habit that your baby is waking up during the night, I suggest trying this method to reset your baby's sleep. Let's say your baby is waking up every night consistently at 3:00 A.M. and your baby is old enough to sleep through the night. Here, you will set your alarm for one hour before baby usually wakes up. In this case, it would be 2:00. Then go to your baby and stir your baby slightly, without waking your baby. This could be rubbing your baby's hair, touching the baby's arm or even lifting it slightly. Even the door creaking when you enter the baby's room might do the trick. You want to do something to make your baby wiggle, flinch a little, or move a little. This will put your baby into a deeper state of sleep, and thus the baby is less likely to wake up at 3:00. If your baby is waking up multiple times a night, I suggest trying this each time. You need to do this 3-5 nights in a row and then the baby will have formed a new habit of sleeping all night. You can do the same thing if baby is waking up really early in the morning and you would like to push their wake time to later. Let's say your baby is waking up at 5 A.M. and you wish the baby would sleep until closer to 8:00. Here, you would follow the same strategy at 4 A.M.

Sometimes this might not work. Then, I suggest letting your baby cry and settle himself again. It might be hard to hear your baby cry, but I would stick to my guns and hold off from giving a bottle. If you feel better, you can always sneak into his bedroom and check to make sure nothing is wrong. If you can do this without him seeing you, that would be even better. The reason is that if he sees you, he will cry even harder, and then it will make it harder for you to hear him cry. You can also use the "distract to relax" method and help your baby settle again. I would try to help your baby sleep again without picking the baby up because then it will be harder to put the baby down again. Of course, if you feel something is wrong, or the baby seems sick, you want to take care of the baby no matter what.

You will probably have to do this for at least three nights before your baby will sleep soundly and doesn't wake up during the night. Also, be sure his bedroom is as dark as possible. This will allow melatonin to relax his brain to help him fall asleep quicker. Of course, if your baby is sick, or something else could be wrong, I suggest you check on your baby.

In my experience, if your baby was sleeping through the night and then suddenly quit sleeping through the night, it's probably just a bad habit. This often happens if your baby has a growth spurt, and they are waking up during the night for a feeding. This is normal if your baby is going through a growth spurt because your baby needs a lot more calories during this phase. However, it is not normal for your baby to continue waking up during the night after the growth spurt is over. Then it might take some crying to help him break the habit.

However, even if your baby was never sleeping through the night before, it can still be because of a bad habit. I would still try the recommendations above.

If your baby never sleeps, well, no matter if it is during the day or during the night, I suggest your baby might have a tongue, lip, or cheek tie. These mouth ties create so many problems for a baby. That is because these mouth ties affect every part of your baby's body. They create tension from the top of his head to the bottom of his feet. They also affect how well your baby can eat and sleep and cause digestive issues. Then your baby will need to have a simple procedure done to release the mouth ties, called a frenectomy. Your baby might also have tense muscles and may need a body-worker or cranial therapist to release the tension. Some babies need both a frenectomy and cranial therapy to release tension. Keep reading, and I will explain this further.

### How to Effectively Treat Ear Infections

Ear infections can also cause pain, particularly when you lay him down to sleep. If a baby has an ear infection, laying him down to sleep creates pressure in your baby's ear. My favorite method of eliminating earache is to take a jar and add chopped onion, chopped garlic, cut lobelia herb (don't use powdered lobelia) mullein flowers and chamomile. Fill the jar only 3/4 full. Then fill it with olive oil. The addition of olive oil will fill the rest of the jar. Then, put a tight cap on the jar; a glass pint or quart canning jar and lid works well. Then, place the jar out in the sun to steep if it is warm outside. Other options are to place the jar by a sunny windowsill or simply on your kitchen counter. Leave this for 2-3 weeks and then strain the herbs. Add some vitamin E oil or lavender oil for a preservative. Then slowly pour a couple of drops into your baby's ear.

I usually gather my own mullein flowers. Mullein is abundant and grows wild beside the road in overgrown ditches. It grows to be about 6 feet tall and has yellow flowers that you can pick easily. There are pictures of mullein online to help you identify it. It is best to let your mullein flowers dry for a couple of days before using them to make the above solution. Drying them first eliminates moisture. Water and oil do not mix, and by adding moisture to the olive oil, it can make the ear solution spoil quicker. The mullein flowers, in addition to lobelia and chamomile, seem to help with the pain of an ear infection. The herbs should be available at most health food stores; however, mullein flowers might be hard to find. Mullein leaf is readily available, but the flowers not so much. Or you can scan the codes below to purchase.

**Mullein Flowers**

This code contains an affiliate link. If you make a purchase through this link, I will receive a commission.

Lobelia Herb, Cut

This code contains an affiliate link. If you make a purchase through this link, I will receive a commission.

Chamomile Herb, Cut

This code contains an affiliate link. If you make a purchase through this link, I will receive a commission.

You can also get these herbs at a local health food store.

If you need a quick option, squeezing an onion and using the juice in your baby's ear can relieve the pain as well.

You can also put olive oil on low heat and then add whatever you have available, preferably the onion and/or garlic. Then after 30 minutes or so, strain and cool. Ideally, the garlic and onion should steep for at least 24 to 48 hours, but sometimes you need something quick, especially if your baby is in pain. You can also try just using olive oil and warming it up a little to make it comfortable for your baby. Then put a couple of drops in his ear. There are also various herbal solutions for ear infections available at health food stores. However, if your baby has constant ear infections, this could be a sign of a tongue, lip, or cheek tie or gut issues. Kefir might help if the issues are caused by gut problems.

Another thing to consider, if your baby does not like to lie down, he might have acid reflux-like symptoms. The symptoms of acid reflux can be caused by a tongue, lip, or cheek tie.

### Dealing with Fever

A feverish baby is unpleasant for both baby and mom. Some parents prefer natural methods of bringing their baby's fever down. While fevers can be helpful in helping your baby fight the offending bacteria, they can make it hard for your baby to sleep. My favorite way to bring a baby's fever down naturally is by using the following method. First, you will need either a double boiler or a kettle and a bowl; the bowl needs to fit nicely on top of the kettle. The size of the kettle and bowl or double boiler is dependent on the amount of fever solution you want to make. Obviously, if you want a big batch, you will need big utensils. So just choose accordingly. You will fill the bottom kettle halfway full of water. Then add the following to the bowl that will sit on top of the kettle: chopped onions, chopped garlic, cut lobelia herb, and cut chamomile herb. Then, add olive oil to the herbs and place the bowl on top of the kettle with water. Then, turn the burner on to the lowest setting. The water in the bottom kettle will warm up, and this will warm up the oil and herbs as well. You want the herbs to be nicely saturated with oil. You can add more oil or herbs if you need to. Keep the burner turned on for anywhere from 1 to 12 hours to allow the herbs to steep into the oil. It is very important that you keep the burner turned on to the lowest setting so as not to overheat the oil. You can also use a thermometer to check the temperature of your oil; 95° to 110° is about the right temperature for your oil to be while steeping. After 1 to 12 hours, allow the oil to cool, then strain, and add some lavender essential oil, peppermint oil. Add vitamin E oil for a preservative. Now the oil solution is medicinal and ready to use.

There is another option to make the fever solution. Here, you will add the chopped garlic, chopped onion, lobelia, and chamomile to a jar. Then, you will pour olive oil over the herbs and the garlic and onion. You will want to add enough oil so that the herbs are nicely saturated with oil. Be sure not to fill the jar more than 2/3 full of herbs and garlic and onion. Then, you cap the jar and let it sit on your counter or put it outside in the sun to steep. Obviously, if it is summer and it is warm, this should work well. You can also just put it on your windowsill by a sunny window to steep. Then steep it for 2 to 4 weeks, strain, and add lavender and peppermint essential oil for a preservative. You can also add vitamin E oil as a preservative. Then it is ready to use. You can also add beeswax pastilles to make it into a salve. Here, you would place the solution over low heat and add beeswax in a ratio of 1 part beeswax to 4 parts oil solution. (Adding more beeswax makes the salve harder; less makes it softer.) Stir the oil solution as the beeswax is melting. Beeswax is like butter; it melts into the oil once warm. Once the beeswax is melted and dissolved, pour the solution into a jar. It will firm up nicely as it cools.

I usually apply this to my baby's spine and on the bottom of her feet and then put her socks on.

You don't need to use specific amounts of herbs or garlic and onion. I have made this solution with no recipe several times, and every time it worked well. However, adding more lobelia than chamomile might be helpful because lobelia really is a star player in this formula.

## When Overstimulation Happens

Despite your best efforts at keeping your baby's environment calm and preventing overstimulation and over-tiredness for the baby during the day, your baby might still be overstimulated and fussy by evening. Sometimes, your baby might just want to be held and cuddled in the evening. Some evenings I would just sit and hold my baby until she slept, and I could not even lay her down without her crying excessively. In that case, a pacifier might be a lifesaver. It's okay to deviate from the daytime routine because evening crying can be stressful. Putting your baby in a sling can help calm and relax them sometimes. Do whatever works for you and your baby. However, during the day, try to maintain the routine and habits you've established. Keep in mind that this won't last forever. Usually by at least 4-1/2 months, the evening fussiness will be gone.

If your baby is overstimulated, especially if they are past the new-born stage, at times it is best to let your baby cry a bit. Sometimes by evening a baby just needs to release some tension, and letting them cry for a bit seems to help your baby relax.

It seems to work similarly for babies as it does for adults. We all know how it feels to have a good cry to release tension and stress. Afterwards, your mind feels more relaxed.

Your baby will occasionally be stimulated by things that are un-avoidable. Let's say you went to a girl's party for lunch and your baby didn't get her usual naps in. Also, your girlfriends were so enamored with your little charmer that they talked excessively to your baby, and now your baby is not only overstimulated but also overtired. Then, I get home, and I try to lay her in her crib, and of course, she just cries.

In my experience, if I try to keep them from crying, they cannot release the built-up tension and stress hormones. Then, I will have a fussy baby for the rest of the day. However, if I just let them cry a bit in their crib, they will be so much happier for the rest of the day. Of course, you can always go in and check on them, but I found out it's best not to distract them too much and just let them release it all. Depending on the amount of overstimulation they had and how overtired they are, it can take a bit for your baby to cry and be able to release it. You can hear as they are winding down and relaxing.

A newborn baby has a harder time relaxing when overstimulated; crying might overstimulate them further. However, once they're a few months old, letting them cry a little can actually relax them. Listen to the cries and figure out what your baby needs. If their crying gets progressively harder, they likely need something or need you to hold them to calm down. This is more common in newborns. If they cry really hard initially but then calm down, they probably just needed to release tension.

**How to Breastfeed to Maximize Your Breastmilk Production**

If you are breastfeeding, it's important to breastfeed on both breasts at every feeding, if possible. The more often you breastfeed, the more you will stimulate your breasts to make more milk. This enables you to maintain your milk supply. It's best to nurse on one side till your breast is empty, then nurse on the other side. That way, your baby will at least get the hind milk from one breast. The baby might not empty the second breast, and that's fine.

An exception to this would be if you have too much milk. This might be true when you have a lot of extra milk coming in and you are engorged. Then you don't want to stimulate your breasts to make more milk. Sometimes just nursing on one side allows your milk supply to slow down a little. However, unless you constantly have too much milk for your baby, breastfeeding on both sides is recommended to help you maintain your supply.

**What to Do for a Sleepy Newborn Who Does Not Eat Well**

Newborn babies can get very sleepy while breastfeeding and may struggle to stay awake for the entire feeding. Here, they will breastfeed for a short time, then fall asleep. My baby would often empty one breast and then be too sleepy to feed on the other side. Then the baby won't be full enough to sleep well. She will also take only brief naps, because she will be hungry so soon again. You can try burping her and see if that wakes her enough to enable her to nurse on the other side. However, since breast milk is so relaxing and some babies are extra sleepy, burping might not always wake her enough for her to continue nursing. Here, you might need to do a different routine. I would breastfeed only on one side first. Then I would burp my baby, then change the baby's diaper. This will awaken the baby enough to enable her to nurse on the other side as well. Since she is so sleepy, the diaper change will not prevent her from falling asleep again. Also, feeding her again after the diaper change allows her to relax before you place her in her crib. I had to use this method a lot because my newborn was so sleepy.

If this routine works better for you and your baby, even as your baby grows older, there's no need for you to switch to the other routine I explained earlier. The primary goal is to have your baby relaxed by the time she is ready for bed. If you can accomplish this using this routine and you prefer this routine, that's okay. Do whatever works for you.

However, I have discovered as my baby gets a couple of weeks/months older; she becomes more awake during feedings. Then, a diaper change between feedings might be too much stimulation too close to bedtime. Therefore, she might have a harder time falling asleep, so you may need to switch to the routine I outlined in Chapter 4 and change her diaper as soon as she wakes up. Again, do what works best for you and your baby.

During the night, when your baby wakes up, she will often be hungry and cry if you don't feed her first. Since it is dark, and that enables her to fall asleep easily again, I will usually feed her on one side and then change her diaper and then feed her on the other side. That way, she's not crying until I finish changing her diaper. She usually had no problem falling asleep with this routine as long as her room stayed dark to enable her to fall asleep again. You can also try red light lamps and bulbs at night when you feed because those help babies fall asleep quicker as they don't inhibit melatonin as much.

If your baby is overly sleepy, this can be a sign of a tongue tie. This is especially true if the problem continues beyond the newborn stage. The last chapters in this book will have more information about a very sleepy baby during breastfeeding and how a tongue tie can cause it.

### How to Fix Your Baby's Day/Nighttime Confusion

You don't want your baby to sleep too long during the day and not get enough feedings in. Then they will wake more at night to feed. This can also cause them to get their daytime and nighttime mixed up. Then they will want to sleep more during the day and be awake more at night. If they sleep longer than 2 hours during the day, you'll want to wake them so this doesn't happen. However, since their eating and sleeping patterns will change the older they get, this is only true for the first six months or so.

You will also want to keep their room bright, ideally with natural light during the day. This will help, because it will keep their feedings in sync with their circadian rhythm.

When it is getting dark outside in the evening, you want it dark inside for your baby as well. This will help your baby relax as she gets ready for her nighttime sleep. Of course, you need some lighting. I usually dim the lights as much as I can while still enabling me to see.

When your baby wakes for a night feeding, be sure to keep the room as dark as possible when you change her diaper, feed, burp, etc. This will help her go back to sleep more easily because you are enabling melatonin in her brain to keep her relaxed. If you need a small nightlight, that is fine. Just try to stay away from overhead and/or really bright lights. Red lights can be really helpful in this case.

In addition, you will want to keep nighttime feedings unengaging and quiet to help the baby readily go back to sleep.

If your baby does fuss after you place her back in her crib, it normally won't last long, especially if her room is dark. Usually, melatonin makes it easier for a baby to fall asleep.

## Acid Reflux

Acid reflux is no fun. If your baby is screaming and in pain, it is frustrating for you as well. However, there are solutions for it below.

Acid reflux can be caused by a tongue, lip, or cheek tie. Mouth ties inhibit proper feeding, and as a result, a baby cannot properly extract milk. An infant needs to be able to maintain a tight seal around the nipple, no matter if you are breast-feeding, or bottle feeding. However, ties inhibit a tight seal around the nipple because of the restriction they cause in the mouth. The loose seal during feeding allows excess air to escape into the baby's tummy when she is eating. These trapped air pockets cause excess spit-up and/or acid reflux.

If your baby is struggling with acid reflux or other symptoms, it may be due to a tongue, lip, or cheek tie. Tongue and lip ties are congenital conditions that occur when the strip of skin beneath a baby's tongue (lingual frenulum) or the upper lip (labial frenulum) is unusually tight, restricting the natural movement of these structures. This condition can significantly affect various aspects of a baby's development and well-being. Mouth ties are often overlooked and misdiagnosed, leading to much frustration for both mom and baby.

It is best to have your baby evaluated by a professional who has training in oral function and can identify ties. If you scan the code below and scroll up until it reads "type in your city or zip code." If you enter your city or zip code, and then select "Go" it will direct you to experts in tongue and lip tie revision in your specific area. These will mostly be dentists. I suggest you take your baby there for an evaluation. These dentists can also correct the ties leading to relief for your baby (and you!)

Tongue Tie Specialists Near Me

It would also be recommended to take your baby to a cranial sacral therapist/body worker in your area. You can search online for cranial sacral therapists or pediatric chiropractors. Cranial therapists work with a baby's fascia, which is a connective tissue right under the skin. If this is tight, it causes pain for your baby and can contribute to acid reflux. A baby who has mouth ties often has muscle tension as well, both from the tongue tie and from other issues, and a cranial therapist is very helpful for this. As a Christian, I try to stay away from cranial therapists who perform Reiki or new age practices. In chapters 9-15, I will explain ties in detail.

There is a yogurt recipe that has gained popularity on the internet because of its effectiveness. The recipe comes from Dr. William Davis, a gut health expert. It is called L-Reuteri Yogurt. L-Reuteri is an essential bacterium that is missing in the gut of most people, especially in the U.S. because of the use of glyphosate and antibiotics. Interestingly, years ago, L-Reuteri probiotics proved helpful for colic in babies. In addition, babies had less spit-up, and infants recovered faster from post-antibiotic diarrhea. Dr. William Davis began studying this crucial strain of bacteria and came up with this recipe. This yogurt has proved amazing for adults as well. People report sleeping better. I experienced more energy and a better mood while on it. L-Reuteri increases neurotransmitters and oxytocin in the body. I will include the recipe here because it may be effective if breastfeeding moms take it for better sleep for their babies and better gut health. Since it is made from pasteurized milk, I recommend caution in giving it directly to an infant, especially premature and newborn babies since premies have an underdeveloped stomach and pasteurized cow's milk can be fatal to them. Ideally, mom can breastfeed and baby gets it through her milk, or the probiotic (not the yogurt) is added to the formula.

Dr. Davis recommends using half-and-half instead of milk. This makes it thicker in texture when cultured. I have used only milk mostly, but think half-and-half is superior to get more cream and fat especially for babies. You could also use milk and add more cream. It needs to be pasteurized milk and cream or half-and-half for it to work. If you have raw milk, heat to 195°F for 10 minutes, then cool it to around 100°. Temperatures above 110° will kill the L-Reuteri. You need a yogurt maker because it needs a consistent temperature for 36 hours to culture into yogurt. Also, sterilize all utensils and containers before starting. I wash all my dishes that I will use in hot soapy water first. This is important to prevent cross-contamination of unwanted bacteria. If that happens, the yogurt can get an unpleasant taste. Inulin is a prebiotic fiber that is needed to help the L-Reuteri culture populate.

**L Reuteri Yogurt**

8 cups half-and-half or milk
1 tablespoon Inulin
1 capsule L-Reuteri probiotic

Warm half-and-half or milk to around 100°. In a small bowl, add 1-2 tablespoons of this liquid, 1 tablespoon of inulin and 1 L-Reuteri capsule. Stir to dissolve. Once dissolved, add to the rest of the milk. Then put in a yogurt maker for 36 hours at 97-100°. Be aware that eating too much can cause diarrhea. I typically eat only 1-1/2 tablespoons at a time to prevent this. I give my young daughters less, or they get diarrhea. You can go to Dr. William Davis' website, www.drdavisinfinitehealth.com, and learn more about this incredible yogurt. He also has some other recipes, including spore-based probiotic yogurt that I have made with excellent results.

# CHAPTER 7
# Routine Changes

As your baby gets older, he will become more awake and alert. Therefore, he might fuss a little after he's put in bed. However, it's usually not excessive. The more consistent you have been at maintaining a specific bedtime routine, the more your baby has learned the habit of falling asleep in his crib. As he gets older, crying will not overstimulate him as much. Therefore, I usually let him settle down for a couple of minutes by himself. You can tell if your baby is only settling himself for a nap by his crying pattern. If he cries, but the crying slows down, he is just settling himself. However, if the crying intensifies, your baby either needs something or is overstimulated. I suggest that if the crying intensifies, to still wait a couple of minutes and see if he's winding down. The older your baby gets, the better it is to let your baby settle himself if possible, rather than intervening. The reason is that, as mentioned before, the older they get, the more awake and alert they become. Then, when you enter their room, your baby will suddenly be wide awake. He's like, "Mom is here, let's play!" Your presence will excite your baby. Then it's harder for your baby to relax again, and your baby will get overtired more easily. Of course, if you are more comfortable always soothing your baby to sleep, that's your choice. Also, if your baby seems to need something, you will want to check on him. Sometimes they have a soiled diaper that needs to be changed, and that prevents them from sleeping.

As they get older, their routine will also start to change. They will be able to handle more activity, and eventually they will want playtime before bedtime. Playtime is not engagement. Playtime consists of a quiet activity where the baby is simply observing his surroundings. You want very little stimulation yet for your baby. Often, I would simply lay my baby on the floor and let him look around. Some three-month-old babies might be ready for playtime; other babies might be closer to four months before they are ready for playtime. Every baby is different; you will be able to tell whether your baby is ready for playtime by observing his cues.

You can always try playtime for a bit before you place them in bed and see how easy it is for them to fall asleep afterwards. If they still fall asleep readily, they are probably ready. Excessive crying will be your sign that it was still too much for them. I would try small increments of playtime first, like 5 minutes or more, and continue adding longer activity times as they grow older. You will still want to place them in bed before they show signs of tiredness, or they will have a really hard time falling asleep.

However, if your baby still has evening fussiness yet, I would try to put your baby in his crib to sleep right after a feeding during those evening hours. Otherwise, playtime might be too much activity for him to manage, and it might turn into crying. Once your baby is no longer battling fussy spells in the evening, you may add some playtime after feeding.

As a baby's nervous system matures even more, the baby will eventually want engagement in addition to playtime during wake times. Engaging with a baby involves communicating with her in fun ways, such as talking, laughing, and tickling. If you have other children, especially young children, they may play and interact with the baby as well, and the baby will enjoy it. Like playtime, you will gradually increase the length of wake time and engagement as your baby matures and is ready for it.

I have found that it is better to engage with your newborn to four-month-old baby before feeding. After four months, you can engage with her throughout the entire wake time. The wake time includes the diaper change, feeding time and just before bedtime. However, every baby is different. Maybe your baby is ready for some engagement throughout her wake time and just before bed-time soon after three months old.

I hesitate to give exact time frames for when your baby will be ready for playtime or engagement. I was always very attentive to my baby's cues, and therefore, I do not remember exactly how old my babies were when I started giving them playtime or engage-ment. The most important thing is that you become your baby's detective and read their cues to determine when they are ready, and not necessarily how old they are.

At some point, babies will want toys to play with during playtime and engagement, and it will not be overstimulating for them. Usually, once they grab for things, they are ready for something to play with. At first, you can give them something as simple as a burp towel or an unused toothbrush, and they will enjoy it. Babies love things they can put in their mouths. Eventually, as they are able to tolerate it, they can also play with toys that sing, or make loud noises. These toys are more stimulating, obviously, but your baby will enjoy them. That is, considering you monitor their cues to determine when they are ready for stimulating toys.

It is important to understand that playtime is much less stimulat-ing than engagement, even for older babies.

My oldest daughter loves playing with her baby sister. She will hold her in her lap and pretend she's her doll. She will talk to her and show her the toys she's playing with. While my baby is at the age (6 months) where this kind of engagement is fine and not too over-stimulating, this will make her tired much quicker than playtime alone. If my baby just plays with toys and has little interaction with people, she can play much longer before becoming tired.

Don't get me wrong, engagement is very important for your baby. Babies need human interaction to mature properly. That is, when given at the right time, and not more than a baby can handle. Babies have the sweetest, charming smiles, so who could resist!

As they get older, the things that were stimulating and overwhelm-ing before will become enjoyable for your baby. Monitor your child's face for signs of tiredness or overstimulation and adjust accordingly. If they smile and love the engagement, you are usually okay. If they keep looking away, not looking back, or start crying, then it is too much.

The older they get, the less you will have to worry about creating a calm environment, and they will want more and more stimulation and excitement. So, adjust accordingly.

Eventually, baths will be far less stimulating, and you will be able to bathe them during the day, and your baby will be fine. Also, they will still only hold eye contact for a short time, but they will show interest in continuing the conversation by looking back at you in anticipation.

In fact, as they get older, if I do not provide enough stimulation or ample playtime and put them to bed too soon after a feeding, they will not take long naps. That is because they are actually 'under tired' and 'under-stimulated.' In this case, all you need to do is adjust their wake window.

Eventually, as they can tolerate even more activity just before bedtime, I will switch the routine up a little more. At some point, I will start changing their diaper before they sleep instead of after they wake up. Since their nervous systems has developed more, they will still be able to fall asleep in the crib on their own, even if they had stimulation before you place them in their crib. Of course, if your baby wakes up with a soiled diaper, you want to change it right away. If this happens, I suggest changing their diaper right away after the baby wakes up and again right before bedtime.

I'm reluctant to give a specific timeframe for when changing their diaper won't affect their sleep. For some babies, it might be as soon as four months. You can learn to detect how much engagement your baby can handle before bedtime and when a diaper change is okay. If I put my baby to bed after a diaper change, and she has a harder time falling asleep without crying excessively, it was too much stimulation for her. Of course, if they make a big poopy mess, you will definitely want to change their diaper before bedtime, no matter what.

Eventually, nighttime or early morning feedings don't mean you cannot engage with your baby anymore. Again, you will be able to tell if your baby can handle stimulation during the night and still be able to sleep afterward. Besides, with their charming smiles and chubby cheeks, it's sometimes too tempting not to interact with them.

Screen time and blue light are detrimental to the maturity of a young child, no matter the age. Therefore, I don't recommend adding screen time at any age. However, if you decide to introduce screen time, I recommend waiting until your child is two years old.

As they continue growing older and adapting, your routine will probably change, especially as they begin eating. Usually, by the time my baby is 7 months old, I am not strictly following a routine. Whenever the baby is hungry, he eats, and when he is tired, he sleeps. The baby's nervous system has matured so much that changes in routine will not affect him much.

To recap, below is an example of the changes in routine as your baby matures.

## The 4 Stages as a Baby Matures

| 1 | 2 | 3 | 4 |
|---|---|---|---|
| Eye contact/ engagement. Diaper change. Eat. Naptime.<br><br>(The amount of engagement is age dependent. Newborns want less engagement than an 8 week old baby, for example.) | Engagement. Diaper change. Eat. Playtime. Naptime.<br><br>The amount of playtime is determined by the baby's age/readiness. Length of playtime is increased as baby can tolerate it. | Engagement. Diaper change. Eat. Engagement in addition to playtime. Naptime.<br><br>Can add engagement during entire wake time in addition to playtime. Can add toys. | Engagement Eat. Playtime/ engagement. Diaper change. Naptime.<br><br>Engagement/play time during wake time. Baby can now have diaper change just before bedtime. |

# CHAPTER 8

# Tips To Lessen Teething And/or Flu Symptoms

WHEN YOUR BABY TEETHES, she will become fussier and sometimes become constipated or get diarrhea. For my first baby, I was giving her formula when she was teething, and she would get high fevers and diarrhea. It was always a stressful experience for me.

I decided I wanted to try implementing kefir in our diet and started giving her kefir. After that, I noticed she had no more teething troubles, no fever, diarrhea, etc. So I switched from formula to kefir, and I never again had any teething troubles with her. I did the same for my next baby, and again there were no teething problems if my babies had kefir daily. My girls got their two-year molars with ease. I never realized they were teething at all.

My girls had a hard time with formula, anyway. Their gut didn't seem to do well with cow's milk or yogurt, yet kefir created no problems for them. While yogurt and kefir both contain probiotics, kefir contains substantially more and a wider variety of probiotics than yogurt.

I have found it helpful to implement kefir in my baby's diet around the time they begin to eat. For my babies, this is usually anytime between five and six months. It takes some time for your baby to adjust to the flavor. In my experience, giving it to your baby when she is really hungry will make it easier for her to consider the kefir and adjust to the taste. However, if your baby has eaten her favorite foods first, she probably won't even consider tasting kefir because she's not overly hungry and has been filled up with other foods. Sweetening it will help. Maple syrup is usually my go-to sweetener, but you can use other sweeteners. Just don't use honey.

It's best to give your baby kefir before the teething problems actually start. If that hasn't been the case, I've found that adding a bit of blackstrap molasses to kefir can help my baby recover more quickly from teething issues. I would add about 1/4—1/2 teaspoons of blackstrap molasses to one cup of kefir. You want to be sure it is only blackstrap molasses because that contains more minerals.

Homemade kefir will give you the best results. You can follow the same guidelines I outlined before to make milk kefir.

I do not recommend using low-fat milk to make kefir. Separating the cream from the milk produces low-fat milk. Cream contains vitamin D, and a baby needs vitamin D to aid teething. Raw, grass-fed milk from a Jersey cow will be your best option. Again, Jersey cow's milk contains higher amounts of cream than other cow's milk. However, do your best to find raw, sustainably sourced, whole milk.

If you decide to buy kefir, be aware, most kefir is made from low fat, pasteurized milk. Therefore, it might not work as well for your baby's teething problems. At one time, I bought kefir for my baby. It was low-fat and made from pasteurized milk. By now you know how essential saturated fat is for a baby's brain, and how it helps their brain to relax. Because of the lack of fat in the milk, she had a much harder time falling asleep. Not only did she lose weight, she became much more fussy. She also had a stomach reaction from it because she would get a rash on her bottom. I suspected it was because of the pasteurization, and that made the milk in the kefir harder to digest. When I switched to homemade kefir made with unpasteurized, whole milk with cream, she started gaining weight again. Her fussiness went away; she was much more content, and she had a much easier time falling asleep. Her rash also disappeared on her bottom. In fact, she preferred homemade kefir to store-bought kefir. After I gave her homemade kefir and switched to store-bought, she refused the bottle at first. She had to be quite hungry before she would take the bottle of store-bought kefir. This may also have been why she lost weight with the store-bought kefir. I could tell she didn't like the taste, nor how it made her feel.

I would not limit the amount of kefir my girls could drink, especially when they were at the teething age. I noticed that one of my babies when she was drooling she would ask for more kefir. I felt like her body was craving the vitamins and minerals, so I would give her more. It was much easier to give her more kefir than to deal with fever and sickness from teething.

Kefir contains high amounts of calcium, magnesium, phosphorus, and potassium. I believe this is why it is so helpful for teething babies.

Since kefir is thicker in texture than formula, you will want a bottle nipple with a bigger hole than what you use for formula or milk. I like the Evenflow botles.

And just for context, I am not a doctor, and this information is for educational purposes only. This information is not intended to diagnose, treat, cure, or prevent any disease. Consult with your doctor before making any changes to you or your baby's diet.

If your baby does not feel well, or is sick, she will become overtired even sooner. If my baby is sick, I am usually very restrictive with playtime. That is because over-tiredness weakens their immunity even more. It also makes it so much harder for them to fall asleep, because not only are they overtired, but they are also not feeling well.

## How to Relieve Your Baby's Cough/Congestion That Hinders Her Sleep

If your baby has a lot of congestion, and that is inhibiting her sleep, I love to use the deep tissue salve. Deep-tissue salve is quite potent. In my experience, deep tissue salve works better than any other menthol-based product or chest rub that I have tried. It is quite strong, so you will want to use it with caution, especially if your baby is a newborn. I usually apply this salve to my baby's upper chest and neck. If there is a lot of congestion, I will also put it along her spine, down the middle of her back. However, be sure to keep it away from her eyes or they will burn. If my baby is newborn, I will apply a carrier oil like coconut oil or castor oil first, then I will apply the deep tissue salve on top. If you have a salve lying around that is gentle, you can use that instead of the coconut or castor oil. Another option would be to first apply the Junior's Bedtime Lotion that I mentioned before, then apply the deep tissue salve on top. The magnesium in the Junior's Bedtime Lotion can help your baby's inflamed chest and neck muscles to relax. By using both the Junior's Bedtime Lotion and the deep tissue salve, you can help your baby relax while relieving congestion at the same time. You can use whichever method works best for you, or you may just want to apply another salve, lotion, or oil before applying the deep tissue salve since deep tissue salve is very strong. This is a more gentle approach, yet powerful enough to loosen your baby's congestion so she can sleep.

Once your baby is like 6 months or older, you can usually apply the deep tissue salve without applying a barrier in between, like lotion, oil or salve. However, some children have sensitive skin, so applying a barrier may be necessary regardless of their age.

You can scan the QR code below with a smartphone camera to purchase deep tissue salve from Nature's Warehouse.

You can also purchase this salve from New Light Health at 717-692-3500.

If you do not have the deep tissue salve, or if you have run out, you can also mix coconut oil with a couple drops of peppermint, eucalyptus, and thyme, or frankincense essential oil. Myrrh essential oil is also antibacterial and would be great to add as well. Another option would be to mix coconut oil with a couple of drops of Breathe oil from dōTERRA. Breathe contains a combination of essential oils to relieve congestion. Either way you decide to make this, you will apply this in the same way as the deep tissue salve. I call this my coconut oil combo. If you don't have coconut oil on hand to make the coconut oil combo, but you have castor oil, that can work well too. Here, you would simply add the essential oils to castor oil, mix, and apply. Castor oil can penetrate deeply and relieve congestion.

If the congestion persists after applying either the deep tissue salve or the coconut oil combo, I suggest using an essential oil diffuser. The oils that I like to use in the diffuser are peppermint, eucalyptus, thyme, and frankincense. Or you can use dōTERRA's Breathe oil. Some diffusers need water to diffuse the oil in the room. However, others are waterless. I have found that the waterless ones work best for this purpose. The waterless diffusers spray a fine mist of undiluted essential oil in the room, and this is more effective at opening your baby's sinuses. Then the sinuses can drain, and your baby can breathe better. I use a diffuser only if the deep tissue salve or coconut oil combo could not open her sinuses and control the congestion. That is because by diffusing the oils into the room, you will use a lot more essential oil. However, if you use a salve, you are applying it directly to your baby, and this is less expensive than buying a lot of oils only to evaporate them in a room. However, on some nights when my baby simply couldn't sleep because of congestion, even after applying salves, my diffuser came in handy. I could also fill the diffuser with essential oil and plug it into the outlet in her room without waking her. If I had applied more salve, I would have had to wake her up. Also, by this time, I was exhausted from being up all night with a coughing baby, and was ready to try anything so the baby could get some sleep.

The diffuser was able to relieve the coughing and congestion, and then we could both sleep. So, do whatever works for you.

Another powerful way to relieve congestion is the steaming method. Here, you will run your shower with hot water. Then you will hold your baby and sit on the inside ledge of the tub facing towards the inside of the bathtub. Obviously, the water is hot, so you will stay far enough away from the running water so it doesn't spray on you or the baby. Then, you will close the shower curtain and allow the steam to open your baby's sinuses and drain the excess congestion. If you only have a shower, you can simply stand inside it, and close the shower curtain and get the same benefits.

### How to Get Hard-to-Reach Snot/Boogers Out of Your Baby's Nose

When a baby has throat congestion, they often have nose congestion as well. Sometimes this inhibits your baby's breathing to where she cannot sleep. Here, the NoseFrida, the Snot Sucker, is a mom's best friend. This is an amazing gadget designed by an ENT to get even the hardest-to-reach snot cleared out of your baby's nose. The NoseFrida has worked to retrieve that sticky snot from my baby's nose better than anything I have tried.

Now to tackle those stuck, annoying boogers in your baby's nose. With my last baby, she had this problem a lot! It was so frustrating, because I had to get the boogers out somehow, or she couldn't sleep. So I would cover her eyes and shine a light in her nose to find the offending booger. Sometimes it was stuck so far back in her nose, I couldn't even see it. If I saw it, it was usually covering up most of the inside of her nostril. This majorly inhibited her breathing, often to where she couldn't sleep. We had a bulb syringe, but that made her nose bleed while I was trying to suction the booger out. NoseFrida to the rescue! The NoseFrida does not need to be put inside your baby's nose, so there's no pain involved for the baby, unlike the bulb syringe. If the boogers are dry and hard, the NoseFrida won't work as well. Here, I recommend using the booger picker. It has a tiny scoop that fits nicely in your baby's nose to get those hard-to-loosen boogers out.

The booger picker only has a limited reach inside your baby's nose. So if your baby has a dried, hard-to-reach booger at the far end of your baby's nose, I recommend filling a nasal syringe with either a saline solution or breast milk. Then slowly add a little into the back of your baby's nose. Allow the liquid to soak into the booger for a couple of minutes, then use the suction power of the NoseFrida to bring the booger to the surface of your baby's nose. When you buy the NoseFrida, you also have the option of buying its saline solution with it. You can also buy a travel case for the NoseFrida. You can buy both the NoseFrida and the Booger picker at Target or scan the QR codes below with your camera.

NoseFrida the Snotsucker

This code contains an affiliate link. If you make a purchase through this link, I will receive a commission.

### SCAN ME

**NoseFrida the Snotsucker Travel Case**

This code contains an affiliate link. If you make a purchase through this link, I will receive a commission.

### SCAN ME

**NoseFrida the Snotsucker With Saline Solution**

This code contains an affiliate link. If you make a purchase through this link, I will receive a commission.

### SCAN ME

**The Booger Picker**

This code contains an affiliate link. If you make a purchase through this link, I will receive a commission.

You can also go to Oogiebear and order the booger picker. You can reach them at 800-959-4548 or email them at customercare@oogiebear.com.

If it is winter, and you have heat circulating through your house, this makes the air dry. Then, your baby breathes the dry air. This can cause the boogers to dry out in your baby's nose and be hard to remove. Here, I recommend running a humidifier in your baby's room to eliminate this.

The next part will be all about tongue, lip, and cheek ties and their effects on a baby.

# CHAPTER 9
# The Effects of Tongue and Lip Ties

THE FOLLOWING INFORMATION MIGHT be the most important you will ever read for you and your child's well-being. In fact, tongue and lip ties can be the root causes behind so many issues that a baby experiences. However, once the tongue and lip ties are reversed through a frenectomy, which is a simple surgery to release the ties, the problems go away.

Tongue, lip, and cheek ties create much frustration for both the mother and baby. Often if a baby has feeding issues caused by a tongue or lip tie, the mom is told her baby is fine. I was told over and over that my baby did *not* have a lip tie.

Mouth ties are tricky to diagnose. Therefore, they are often undetected and misdiagnosed. It's very important that if you feel your baby has the symptoms of a tongue, lip, or cheek tie, that you take them to an expert to get it checked out. Only a professional who has had training in oral function can properly identify and correct a mouth tie; usually, dentists and lactation consultants are the experts at diagnosing mouth ties. However, it is important to understand that not all dentists and lactation consultants have had training to diagnose tongue, lip, and cheek ties.

Many times, when a mom has pain when breastfeeding, she will ask a lactation consultant to evaluate the situation. If the lactation consultant does not have any training in oral function, she will not understand how tongue, lip, and cheek ties affect breastfeeding. Therefore, she will not look in the baby's mouth to determine if any ties are present and are causing the problems. Instead, she will simply instruct the mom to try different feeding positions to feed her baby. However, if a baby has a mouth tie, the position of the baby during breastfeeding does not fix the restriction caused by the mouth tie. Then the mom continues to experience immense breastfeeding pain, but feels it is "all in her head." Some moms simply switch to bottle-feeding. However, the baby continues to have oral dysfunction from her mouth tie.

On the other hand, a lactation consultant educated in oral function will examine the infant's mouth and be able to diagnose any ties. Also, there are many other 'normal' symptoms caused by ties besides painful breastfeeding. Digestive issues are a common problem if a baby has a mouth tie. A lactation consultant who is knowledgeable in oral function will be able to determine if your infant is experiencing other symptoms that may be caused by a mouth tie.

# CHAPTER 10

# What Is a Lip and Tongue Tie?

*What is a Lip Tie?*

A LIP TIE OCCURS when the labial frenulum, the tissue connecting the upper lip to the upper gum, is unusually thick, tight, or extends too far down toward the gum line. Difficulties with breastfeeding, latching, and speech development can arise because of this.

Here are some examples of what a lip tie looks like.

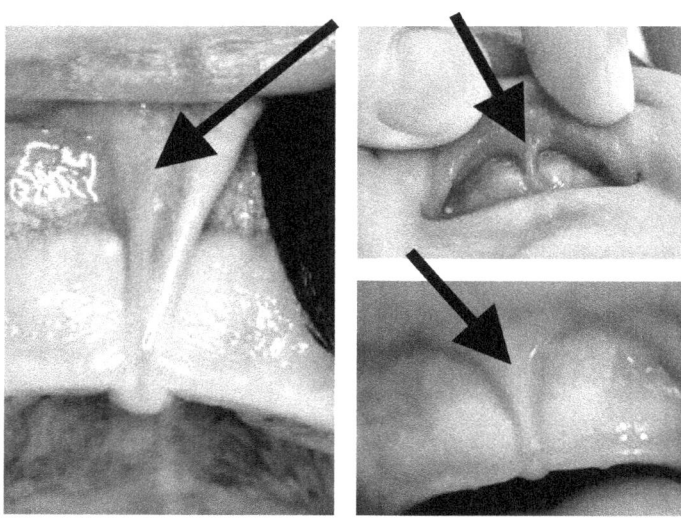

## What is a Tongue Tie?

Tongue tie, also known as Ankyloglossia, is when the tissue connecting the tongue to the bottom of the mouth is too tight or short. Problems can arise, especially with breastfeeding, if the tongue is restricted.

Here are examples of what a tongue-tie looks like. However, there are various forms of tongue ties, and some tongue ties are not as obvious. A posterior tongue tie is more tricky to decipher because the muscle of the tongue is restricted. Therefore, only a professional can diagnose it. Just because you can't visibly see a tight frenum like in the photos below, does not mean your baby does not have a tongue tie.

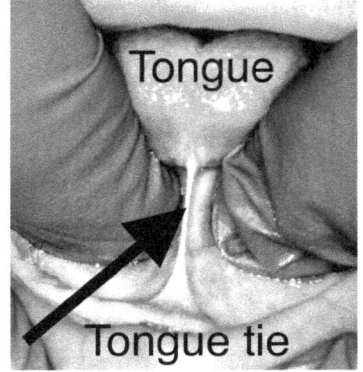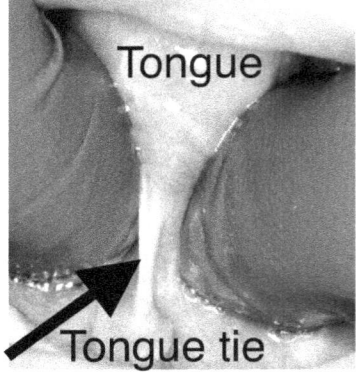

2. Photo credits, Dr. Eilish Welsh, Brunswick KIDDS Pediatric Dentistry

# CHAPTER 11

# Maternal Effects of a Tongue/Lip Tie

THE SIGNS AND SYMPTOMS below show how a baby's mouth tie can affect the mother.

**Maternal Effects of a Baby's Tongue/Lip Tie**

1. Early decrease in breast milk production
2. Nipple damage presenting as flattening, blisters, bruises, cuts, or bleeding
3. Experiencing moderate to intense pain during latch-on attempts
4. Nipple infection or inflammation
5. Engorgement or breasts not being completely drained
6. Mastitis
7. Nipple thrush
8. Blocked milk ducts
9. Early cessation of breastfeeding[1]

When an infant has a lip or tongue tie, they have a shallow latch because of the restricted tongue and/or lip. Then, the baby cannot empty the breast and get to the rich hind milk. This can cause

---

1. Concepts adapted from SOS 4 TOTS, Lawrence Kotlow

a breast infection for a mom because her breast never drains completely. Another symptom can be a decrease in breast milk production. Because of the shallow latch, the infant's suck is insufficient to produce enough stimulation and properly extract milk from a mother's breast. In turn, the mom loses her milk supply.

When I had my first baby, I thought it was normal to struggle with breast infections all the time. I had to stay on some type of supplements just to stay on top of my constant breast infections.

Some mothers report immense pain when breastfeeding if their baby has a tongue and/or lip tie. For my first two babies, I did not have that problem. However, with my third baby, the pain was intense. Thankfully, we knew it was because of a lip tie and scheduled a frenectomy as soon as possible. The frenectomy helped relieve the blistered nipples I got when breastfeeding.

# CHAPTER 12
# Infant's Effects of a Tongue/Lip Tie

Here are the effects a mouth tie has on a baby.

- Difficulty latching

- Falls asleep during feeds

- Reflux or frequent spit-up

- Poor weight gain

- Frequent feeds

- Snoring, heavy or mouth breathing

- Difficulty with pacifier

- Gagging, choking, coughing

- Milk dribbling from the baby's mouth

- Gassiness

- Colic

- Torticollis [1]

- Retained burps

- Takes brief naps

- Wakes constantly at night

- Lying in odd positions when sleeping (i.e. head cranked sharply left, right, or back)

A tongue tie restrains the tongue to the bottom of the mouth. Then the tongue can move neither forward nor up. The problem with this is, the only other place for the infant's tongue to go is in her airway. Then the infant cannot breathe correctly. Therefore, some babies with a tongue tie will gag or choke when you place a pacifier, bottle, or a mother's nipple into their mouths.

Laying a baby with a tongue tie on his back to sleep can make it difficult for the infant to breathe. Therefore, I recommend putting an infant on his tummy to sleep. At the back of this book, by the testimonials, there's a story of an infant who would choke whenever his mom laid him on his back to sleep. For more about this, refer to the last topic in this chapter, below the picture.

This also accounts for infants who will constantly slide off the mother's nipple while breastfeeding. The tongue tie blocks their airway, and the only way they can catch their breath is by unlatching from the breast repeatedly.

The restricted tongue/lip tie causes an insufficient latch/suck. Then, since the baby cannot properly extract the milk, the infant cannot gain properly. Some infants will lose weight as a result.

Sleep apnea and snoring are also major symptoms of a tongue tie. An infant or child should not snore. Again, the tongue is tethered to the bottom of the mouth. This closes off the child's airway and forces them to breathe through their mouth instead of their nose. Sometimes they will snore because of it.

It is important that the tongue rest at the roof of a baby's mouth. This enables the baby to breathe through their nose. A baby should only breathe through their nose. The problem with a tongue tie, a baby's tongue cannot reach the roof of the baby's mouth. This "low-hanging tongue" can cause mouth breathing, especially when sleeping. The picture below shows what mouth breathing looks like. You can see the baby's mouth is open, showing that the baby is breathing through her mouth. This is never a good sign. The lips should be tightly sealed to show that the baby is breathing through her nose instead of her mouth. Sometimes it may even look like they are gasping for breath or gagging. It is very important that a baby has enough oxygen flowing to his brain. This is especially true during the early weeks of the infant's brain and nervous system growth. However, the tongue-tie hampers the much-needed oxygen.

*A baby with a mouth breathing problem, indicating low tongue posture and possible tongue tie.*

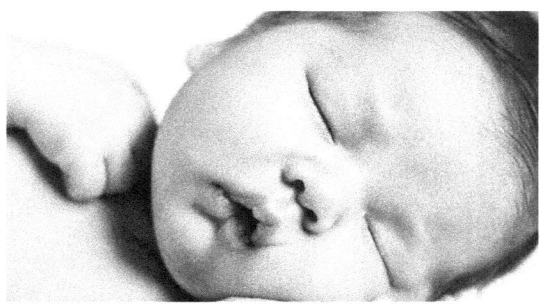

*Another example of mouth breathing.*
*Also note how the bottom lip is pulled in,*
*another example of oral restriction.*

*Here is an example of optimal tongue*
*posture making nose breathing possible.*
*Note lips are tightly sealed, unlike the*
*other two pictures.*

The reality is, a baby who is mouth breathing while sleeping will not be able to get a deep, restful sleep due to the lack of oxygen. A speech-language pathologist (SLP) or myofunctional therapist who has taken training in oral ties can be a wonderful asset as well. If your baby received a release and is still mouth breathing, these two types of professionals are invaluable in correcting this problem. Some myofunctional therapists will not see a baby younger than three, but SLPs will. If you can find a good dentist in your area who understands oral restriction, you can usually call them for referrals. There's more information at the back of this book about how to find a knowledgeable dentist.

Another thing I have observed is that some babies who have a tongue tie are more fussy or have prolonged periods of crying. A reason for this is that a baby's tongue needs to rest at the roof of the baby's mouth. This is soothing to a baby. This is why sucking is comforting for a baby-the tongue strokes the top part of the baby's mouth, relaxing and calming a baby's nervous system. When the tongue cannot reach the top to soothe the baby, you have a fussy baby. At the back of this book, there is a testimonial of a baby who screamed nonstop from 7PM to 12AM every night. After correcting the tongue-tie, the constant crying halted. In fact, the mom commented that after baby came home from a release, baby started sleeping all night from that point on, instead of screaming for hours. She said after the first night of no screaming, she could barely hope this could last. However, soon she realized the nights of baby crying for hours were over.

A baby who can never sleep long stretches ever is one of the biggest red flags for tongue and lip ties that I have seen. In fact, it's the **BIGGEST** symptom I see in babies with ties. That's because a baby with ties, especially a tongue tie, cannot breathe properly. As a result, the baby cannot sleep well. Inside the front cover of this book, you can read a little about a mom's story. Her baby was only sleeping in 10-minute stretches at a time during the day. Sometimes if she got REALLY lucky, baby would sleep 30-minute stretches. However, other times, baby would wake up as soon as she laid baby in the crib and refuse to sleep. Most of the time, her baby only took 10-minute naps. At night, baby would only sleep a one-hour stretch at a time. She tried sleep training, but it simply did not work. Baby would cry for hours and refuse to sleep. When she found me, her baby was 6 months old, and she was exhausted. She told me she was barely sane from sleep deprivation. After listening to her story, I learned she had been to a dentist when baby was 5 weeks old to see if her baby had any ties. The dentist sent her to a lactation consultant, who concluded that there were no ties. Next, she went to a chiropractor, and the chiropractor detected a lip tie and sent a picture of the baby's lip tie to a midwife. The midwife determined that there definitely was a lip tie and snipped the tie with scissors. (In Chapter 14, you can read more about why snipping a tie with scissors is not an effective way to release ties.)

Now, one important thing to note here is that a baby rarely has just a lip tie alone-there is always a tongue tie as well. This is especially true if the baby has sleep issues. The reason for this is, **a tongue tie inhibits proper breathing, and a baby who cannot breathe well cannot sleep well.** It takes a special training for a dentist, or any professional for that matter, to diagnose a tongue tie. Most chiropractors, midwives, pediatricians, and even some lactation consultants do not have the expertise to diagnose a hidden tie because they have no training in oral function. Sometimes the lip tie is the most obvious, but the tongue tie is problematic as well; it just has not been properly diagnosed and corrected.

So when this mom came to me, I recommended she go to a dentist who had proper training to evaluate and correct any possible ties. She ended up going to Dr. Eilish from Brunswick Kidds Pediatric Dentistry, one of the most knowledgeable tongue-tie dentists. Dr. Eilish identified and corrected the tongue tie, and then this mom implemented the baby sleep routine and strategies in the first part of this book. She called me back a couple of months later to tell me her baby was now sleeping 2 hour stretches during the day. In fact, she said sometimes he will sleep such long stretches; she has to wake him up for a feeding. And the best part? Baby was now sleeping 11-hour stretches at night! This mom could have tried a million different things to help her baby sleep better, but until the ties were properly corrected, nothing would have changed. That's because her baby was not only uncomfortable from the ties, but baby also could not breathe well, and that is why it was impossible for the baby to sleep for long stretches.

A baby with a tongue-tie can have a hard time staying awake to eat properly because of the lack of oxygen. My first baby was so sleepy that I could barely get her to breastfeed. Since she kept falling asleep during feeding, she never really got a full tummy. She also never got to the rich hind milk. Then, since she was never satiated, she only took brief naps. Of course, I did not know she had a tongue tie that was causing this.

When my second baby was born, a nurse told us she seemed to have a lip tie. I should've just listened to her and taken her to a professional to get it checked out. Instead, I sought about 8 more opinions from around five different chiropractors and a couple of nurses, a lactation consultant, and they all said my baby was fine. However, I could tell she was not fine. She would seem uncomfortable when I laid her on her back. Finally, one experienced female chiropractor was able to tell me there was something wrong with her cranials. She said they were overlapped and not growing properly.

Also, I would burp her and then put her to bed, and 10 minutes later she would have another burp, and half an hour later she would have yet another burp. This continued day in and day out. Because of these delayed burps all the time, she couldn't sleep well, and she would wake up crying. I didn't realize that her lip tie had anything to do with this. (This is what I call retained burps.)

Finally, we took her to a pediatric dentist, and after an examination; she sent us back home, saying she was okay. She mentioned it wasn't bad enough to warrant immediate action. Something in my mother's heart knew she was wrong.

Next, our baby began losing weight for no apparent reason. So I called my husband's cousin, who had experience with tongue and lip ties because three of her children had them. I told her about the problems we were having, and she advised us to go to a different pediatric dentist. When we got there, this dentist took one look at our baby and said she had a Class 4 lip tie.

Our baby also had a posterior tongue-tie. So, this dentist performed what is called a frenectomy, which involves using a laser to cut the tie. After we had this procedure done, we experienced a transformation in our baby. There were no more delayed burps, and she started gaining weight rapidly. In addition, we took her to a cranial therapist who was able to release the tension in her head from her tight cranial bones. She was also able to release the tightness in our baby's mouth from the tongue and lip tie.

Tongue and lip ties limit a baby's ability to create a tight seal around the mother's nipple when breastfeeding. Because of this, the baby might make a clicking sound when she is breastfeeding. Sometimes milk will dribble out of the side of the baby's mouth because of the loose seal. In addition, the infant will swallow too much air while breastfeeding. After nursing, the baby will have excess air in her tummy. Therefore, a baby cannot get all her burps out of her tummy. If it gets really uncomfortable, a baby will cry excessively. Health professionals often misdiagnose this as acid reflux or colic; however, it is just excess air that is being swallowed.

The same holds true for a bottle-fed baby. The baby cannot maintain a tight seal around the nipple, resulting in a lot of excess air in their tummy.

During birth, a baby's head is flexible in order to move through the birth canal. The cranial bones will overlap to allow the baby's head to flex. However, after birth, a baby's cranial bones need to spread as the baby's head grows. When a baby sucks, the baby's tongue should reach to the top of his mouth. This allows the baby's head to grow and the cranial bones to expand. However, with a tongue tie, the tongue cannot reach the top of the mouth. Then a baby's head cannot grow properly. Therefore, they often need cranial therapy besides a frenectomy. This allows the baby's head to grow properly after a frenectomy. In addition, the baby's head experiences tension when cranial bones overlap and do not grow properly. A cranial therapist can release tension in a baby's head that was created by a tongue or lip tie.

Some parents have reported they have seen only minimal results after a frenectomy. However, after a frenectomy and a cranial treatment from a cranial therapist, they have seen major results. This was true for us as well, with my second baby.

Besides cranial therapy, massage can be helpful in releasing the tension created by a tongue and/or lip tie. The coconut oil rub downs can work wonderfully for this. You can also use your favorite lotion and massage your baby with it. Again, my favorite option would be to use the Junior's Bedtime Lotion instead of coconut oil, because this not only contains coconut oil, but magnesium as well. Magnesium is wonderful for relieving tightness and tension in the body.

One mother reported that besides cranial therapy, massage has been powerful for her baby. She recommended doing it multiple times a day, and at the very least, once a day. Besides having a more relaxed baby, she said her baby could go longer between cranial treatments because of the therapeutic use of massage. If you do it multiple times a day, I would recommend doing it at the same time as you are changing the baby's diaper. That way, the baby will handle the stimulation from the rubdown better.

In addition, mouth ties inhibit many other bodily functions because of the restriction they cause. Because of this, better results can be obtained by taking your baby to a cranial therapist after the frenectomy. Often, more things are wrong than just a tongue, lip, or cheek tie. In addition, if your baby's mouth has been restricted for a while by a mouth tie, her mouth muscles will be tense because of the improper sucking habit. A cranial therapist will adjust and release the tension in your baby's mouth created by the tongue tie.

The best time for any baby to get a frenectomy done is immediately after birth. The longer you wait, the more the baby will have to compensate for the restriction on their tongue. This can lead to the habit of improper sucking. Babies may need extra help to latch and suck correctly after a frenectomy if they've been sucking improperly. A lactation consultant can assist with this.

Also, be aware that tongue/lip ties are often genetic. So usually, if one child has it, they all have it.

It is important to understand that some tongue ties may be more obvious than others. What makes some tongue ties noticeable is they have a tight tissue under the tongue. Then, when someone lifts the tongue, they can easily see the tight tissue. However, a posterior tongue tie is different. With a posterior tongue tie, the muscle of the tongue is actually the problem and needs a release. This is not noticeable at all to someone who has taken no training in oral function. Therefore, only a professional who knows how to recognize a posterior tongue tie can effectively make a diagnosis. While a tongue tie with tight tissue is easier to see, it is still advisable to get it diagnosed by a pediatric dentist. Only a pediatric dentist or someone who has taken training in oral function can tell if the tongue tie is creating any oral or bodily dysfunction.

If a baby has a tongue tie and no frenectomy is done to correct it, sometimes the child will need braces later. This happens because the tongue needs to reach the top of the mouth in order for the jaw to grow and widen properly. Not releasing the ties can cause problems with the child's jaw growth and lead to crowded teeth, requiring braces in the future.

A lip tie can create a problem too. Because of the thick tissue growing down from the upper lip to the gum line, the child's teeth cannot grow together nicely. Instead, there will be a sizeable gap at the front center of the child's mouth where the lip tie is. Here, the child's first teeth will come in with a gap and never be able to grow back together.

Here is a good example of what that problem can look like.

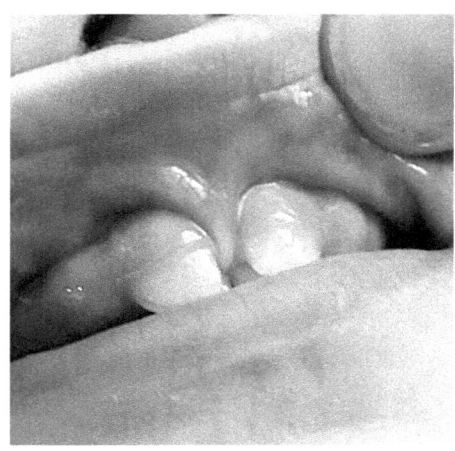

Now, every pediatrician, doctor, labor nurse, lactation consultant, etc. will tell you that you must lay your baby on their back to sleep. No exceptions. That's because they believe laying your baby on her back to sleep causes SIDS (sudden infant death syndrome). In fact, they are legally required to tell you this. The problem is, a baby with a tongue tie cannot sleep well on his back because their airway is already restricted and this makes it worse. Sometimes a baby will even choke after being put on her back to sleep because of lack of oxygen. In fact, if a mom comes to me with a baby that's not sleeping well that I suspect has a tie, I will instruct her to start immediately placing the baby on his tummy to sleep, at least until the tie is corrected.

This is also why some babies will try to flip onto their tummies to sleep, and Mom starts panicking because she's heard a baby should NEVER sleep on her tummy. There's a reason your baby wants to sleep on her tummy. In fact, when a baby is too young to flip to their tummy and they struggle with catching their breath because of a tongue tie, they will sometimes lie in odd positions in an attempt to breathe. Sometimes baby will twist her head to the right, to the left or will crank her head way back. This is a problem, because the poor baby is trying her best to get off her back and get comfortable. In fact, even without a tongue tie, I've yet to see a baby who can sleep as well on her back as on her tummy. In fact, I hear this so often that "My baby wants to sleep on her tummy, but I can't let her." A baby sleeping on her back is about as helpless as a turtle flipped on its back. I recommend reading the article below from joyfulnurturing.com. She is a doula and has reached the same conclusion as I have—babies always sleep better on their tummies. I could not have explained this better than she does in this article.

**Tummy Sleep Article**

It has been proven that placing your baby on her tummy to sleep actually helps your baby's brain develop better. It can also make your baby smarter, because tummy time is critical for proper brain growth. In the article above, she covers why tummy time is crucial for proper development. Since a newborn sleeps so much, it is impossible to get adequate tummy time otherwise. In addition, if you don't put them to sleep on their tummies as a newborn, it can make it difficult for the baby to adapt to tummy sleep and tummy time later.

In the article above, the pediatrician admitted babies are still dying from SIDS even while sleeping on their backs. Years ago, moms were told that it is NOT safe to put their baby on their BACK to sleep.

Breastfeeding can majorly lower your baby's chance of SIDS. Placing a fan in your baby's room can lower the risk as well.

I suggest you do your own research as to the true cause of SIDS and why stomach sleeping is being blamed for it.

As always, it is your decision how you want your baby to sleep. Either way, I am not responsible for the outcome if you decide to lay your baby on her stomach or back to sleep. This information is for informational purposes only, and you should consult with your doctor to make an informed decision. This is not medical advice and is not intended to diagnose, treat, cure or prevent any disease. With that said, it is my legal duty to inform you that the American Academy of Pediatrics recommends babies be put on their backs to sleep to prevent SIDS.

Now, one important thing to note, I am not trying to put down midwives, doula's, pediatricians, chiropractors, lactation consultants, doctors, and dentists who cannot diagnose ties. They have really good intentions. They mean no harm, and I do not wish to make them sound like bad people. What I want to point out is, moms are asking the opinion of these medical professionals when they have no formal training in tongue, lip, and cheek ties and this is where the problems start. Then mom is told baby has no ties, or the tie is not causing any issues. However, when mom goes to a specialist with the right kind of training, the tongue tie specialist identifies and corrects the tie. This makes all the other professionals look bad, when in reality they were asked their opinion on something they had no expertise in. So we can't blame them for their misdiagnose. So here's my point-**don't ask anybody except a properly trained tongue tie specialist to evaluate your baby for any possible ties if you want to know the truth.**

I have recently learned something very interesting from Michelle Emanuel. She is an IBCLC lactation consultant and is an expert on ties in babies. (Yes, there are lactation consultants out there that are well trained and knowledgable about ties.) She stated that babies with oral ties and dysfunction sometimes have what she calls zig zag toes or clenched toes. The first picture below reflects what she describes as zigzag toes, where some toes are up and some are down. The third picture is an example of clenched toes.

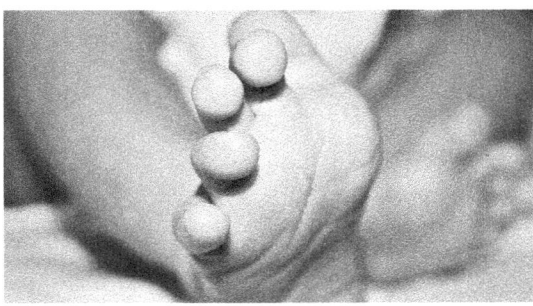

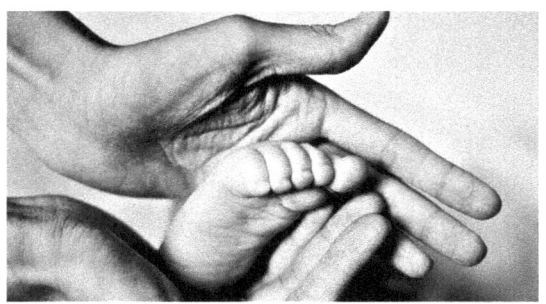

While I have never considered the idea to look at a baby's toes, and most of my clients are from various states and abroad, so I never see the baby, I feel there has to be some truth to it because the tongue is connected to the toes. In this case, the toes are compensating for the tension in the mouth and/or tongue. While I think this can indicate a tie, I don't think you should ONLY look at your baby's toes to determine if a baby has a tie. However, I think it is an interesting part of the puzzle, especially when combined with an evaluation from a properly trained professional. Michelle has a lot of excellent videos on Instagram @tonguetiebabies. Her website is babymyo.com and she is an expert in her field on this topic. If you are in the Cincinnati, Ohio area and looking for a skilled professional to evaluate your baby for ties, she would be a good resource. I will include her contact information in the back of this book. She also has a YouTube channel at Feeding, Breathing, and Being Babies. However it is difficult to find her channel due to the name sounding like a video. So you can scan the code below to find it easily.

2

---

2. Photo credits, Wanita Kuhns

# CHAPTER 13

# Cheek Ties

ANOTHER PROBLEMATIC MOUTH TIE is the cheek tie.

*What is a cheek tie?*

A cheek tie is a term used to describe a condition known as a "buccal tie." Like a tongue and lip tie, it restricts movement in a baby's mouth. The difference is the cheek is tied instead of the tongue and/or lip.

Unfortunately, I do not have any pictures of cheek ties. However, more information about cheek ties, including pictures are available from Dr. Lawrence Kotlow's book, SOS 4 TOTS.

# CHAPTER 14

# Who Can Correct A Tongue And Lip Tie?

IF YOU ARE A parent who sees these signs, you will need to visit a dentist for a professional evaluation of your child's symptoms. You will need to contact them and ask them if they perform frenectomies. Also, you will want to ask the dentist the following questions:

**1.What kind of instrument do they use to do a frenectomy?**

There's one instrument that works safely and effectively for mouth ties, and that is a laser. Some individuals (usually not someone who understands oral function) will try using a scissors and attempt to snip it. However, this is not an effective method. The safety of this method is also questionable; it can cause a lot of bleeding.

**2. Do they teach any post-therapy stretches to keep the site from healing back together again?**

If they do not have this in place, you are wasting your time with them. If no therapy is done afterward, you might as well not do the surgery in the first place because you will need to do it again. This is essential! The reason post-therapy is so important is that the surgical site will want to grow back together. And if no therapy is done, it will. Usually stretches are done 4-6 times a day for 2-6 weeks, depending on the specific dentist's advice. Anything less than that will allow the site to reattach again.

Sometimes, even though you are doing therapy, you might not be doing it correctly, and this enables the surgical site to grow back together again. The dentist that we go to will actually do a post-op checkup about a week later to make sure this is not happening. I think this is very prudent. It tells you a lot about the professional and how well they understand the importance of not allowing the tie to grow back together as it was.

Do you recall the story of when I took my baby to a pediatric dentist who claimed to know about tongue and lip ties, but sent us home with no help? I wasn't a professional by any means, but I could see my baby had a lip tie, and in my heart, I knew she was wrong. So, if you feel something doesn't quite add up, it is always best to get a second opinion.

Some people, including dentists, believe the myth that tongue and lip ties are not serious enough for surgery or that children will outgrow them. They will tell you things like, "There's a little bit of a tie, but not enough to need surgery." Or "Your child will grow out of it." Or the one I heard over and over, "Your baby is fine." If a child has a tongue and/or lip tie that is causing restriction, it is a problem that needs to be addressed. If you don't deal with the ties now, you will need to someday.

If your older child has symptoms that you feel may be related to a mouth tie, I suggest you read the book SOS 4 TOTS by Lawrence Kotlow. This book goes into detail about the effects of mouth ties in older children.

There is a list of knowledgeable dentists who perform frenectomies in the back of this book. You can also search online for dentists who perform frenectomies with a laser and ask them the specific questions above. You can also go to YouTube and in the search bar type in the following: "*Brunswick kidds pediatric dentistry tongue ties.*" Here you can listen to more stories of children who had mouth ties. You can also scan the code below and enter your city and state. These specific dentists that show up have taken training in laser frenectomies; however, I will still ask them if they incorporate any post therapy stretches. If they do not, they are not knowledgeable about mouth ties.

Tongue Tie Specialists Near Me

Note: There is a new therapy coming out that might be helpful for mouth ties called Oralase and BabyLase. Some tongue and lip tie specialists are implementing it. It is using PhotoBioModulation to loosen the muscles and tissues around the frenulum and mouth. Sometimes when there is so much tension in these areas, it can mimic a tie. This is great to use as a first step to see if the need for a frenectomy is eliminated. Sometimes, baby will still need a release, depending on the severity of the case.

# CHAPTER 15
# Testimonials

AFTER THE BIRTH OF *my first baby, I began having problems with breastfeeding. I grew very sore from nursing. It felt like I was being pinched all the time while feeding. My baby would also fuss whenever I tried to nurse. She would unlatch and cry, for no reason. Then, because she was hungry yet, she would try to suck again, and the cycle would continue. She also made a clicking sound while nursing. I felt like something had to be wrong.*

*My husband was explaining the feeding problems our baby had to my brother-in-law. He suggested the possibility of a tongue-tie. We located a pediatric dentist and went to have it checked out. Our baby had a class 2 lip tie, as well as a tongue tie.*

*After the surgery, breastfeeding immediately felt better; I had no more soreness. It took a little for our baby to adapt, but with time, she no longer quit nursing until she was done. Eventually, the clicking sound she had made before went away as well.*

*The best advice I can give to parents is this; if your baby has any symptoms of a tongue or lip tie, get it evaluated by someone who is knowledgeable in identifying mouth ties.*

*Earl and Hannah Miller*

After my 5th baby was born, he would only take brief naps. In addition, I could not lay him down in his crib because he would choke. He would also have spells of fussiness and crying. I became desperate, wondering what was wrong with my baby. My midwife thought it seemed like he had a tongue and lip tie, so we took him to a pediatric dentist. After the evaluation, the dentist diagnosed him with a tongue and lip tie and performed a frenectomy.

When I got home, he slept for six hours. I could also lay him in his bed with no choking. However, I still didn't dare to hope this might have been the answer because I was afraid he would revert back to the crying baby who couldn't sleep again. It seemed too good to be true. I am happy to say I have a much more content baby. After I have got back from the frenectomy, he has slept through the night since.

Our other four children also had various problems, so I took them to a cranial therapist. She identified the issues as being caused by a tongue tie and recommended doing a frenectomy for all four.

Our oldest child had constant digestive issues. She also snored when she slept. Since the frenectomy, the digestive issues have cleared up and her snoring is minimal.

Our son, next in age, couldn't speak clearly. He would also snore when sleeping. Now, his speaking is much better. His snoring has improved as well. After the frenectomy was done, he exclaimed, "My tongue can touch the top of my mouth!"

Our third child had vision problems from the time she was a baby. Her one eye could not focus correctly. Therefore, she would have a lot of falls. At 15 months old, we had to get her glasses to remedy this. Immediately after the frenectomy, none of her eyes could focus. This suggested a connection between her eye problems and her tongue-tie. It got a little better, especially after we took her to the cranial therapist to release some of the tension, but we hope it improves more with time.

Abe and Hannah Petersheim

When my oldest child was born, I had a hard time getting his burps up. He would be fussy because the burps seemed to stay stuck in his tummy. Therefore, he could not settle down well and sleep.

With my second child, I had the same issues. It would take 1 to 2 hours to get all the burps out of his tummy after a feeding. By the time I was done burping, it was time for another feeding. It seemed all I did all day was burp my baby. At night, after his last feeding, I would lay him down in his crib, asleep. However, he continued waking with more burps in his tummy. I had to go to his room repeatedly to burp him. Another issue we were having is, I was breastfeeding, and the milk would flow so fast that he could not keep up. This caused him to slide off the nipple constantly. He also had constipation.

Finally, it was so frustrating to breastfeed my baby because of the problems I had that I switched to formula feeding. However, that did not seem to change anything. I talked to my midwife about the problems I was having with feeding and burping. She said he has a tongue tie, and she thought it might be a good idea to clip it with scissors. However, after snipping the tongue tie, there was only minimal improvement. After three weeks, it was back to how it had been before.

We went to a reunion, and I met a cousin there whose children had problems with tongue and lip ties. She told me she thinks my baby has a tongue-tie. Later, at an auction, I was talking to a midwife and asked her for references to a dentist who could perform a frenectomy for our baby. She referred me to Dr. Mahoney. We took our baby for a frenectomy, and after that his symptoms improved. I had no more problems getting his burps out of his tummy and his constipation problems went away.

When my third baby was born, I again had the same issues with her. Besides not being able to get her burps out of her tummy, she was also a messy eater. I would lay a towel on my lap when she would eat because there would be milk all over by the time she was done. I called a lactation consultant and explained the problems I was having. I asked her if she thinks my baby has a tongue tie. She said she doesn't think there would be a problem with a tongue tie. However, I continued having problems with her feeding. Finally, I took her to a chiropractor, and he identified a tongue tie that was causing the feeding problems. Again, we went to Dr. Mahoney. After the frenectomy, she was no longer a messy eater. She could finally get her burps out of her tummy effectively as well.

We had to go back to Dr. Mahoney for a post-op check up for our baby and this time we also took our oldest child along to be evaluated *for a tongue tie. By this time, he was 2-1/2 years old. Dr. Mahoney performed a frenectomy on him as well. After the frenectomy, I noticed he could speak more clearly than before.*

Jason and Diane Miller

My baby was born at a hospital and the first thing I noticed when my baby latched on to nurse was the terrible pain I had. I pushed it off as "he must really have a strong latch." The hospital staff checked my baby for a tongue tie and concluded that there was none. Later I went to my chiropractor, and she thought it looked like a lip tie for sure, but no tongue tie. We made an appointment with a pediatric dentist. At his office, he diagnosed my baby as having a class 4 lip tie. He also had a posterior tongue tie. (Note: from the author. Here is a good example of why it is so important to only let a professional who has had training in oral function to diagnose any mouth tie, especially a tongue tie. This chiropractor could identify the lip tie. However, a tongue tie can be so tricky, especially a posterior tongue tie.)

After the frenectomy, I could tell a big difference in the amount of pain I used to have when breastfeeding. The discomfort was very minimal and came mainly from the bruising that had occurred before the frenectomy. It felt so different to actually breastfeed without agony and pain.

*The best advice I would give to other parents who suspect their baby has a mouth tie would be this. When in doubt, get it checked out! We have older children, and we did not get them checked for a mouth tie when they were a baby. Now I wish we would have.*

*Verlin and Rachel Herschberger*

After my baby was born, she seemed to breastfeed well at first. However, with time, breastfeeding became very frustrating for both me and the baby. After a short time of nursing, she would swallow air. Then, she would cough and cry. Then she would try to nurse again, and the cycle continued. Finally, she would get frustrated and quit nursing shortly after starting. However, I knew she had not nursed long enough to be full. Her brief and unsatisfying feedings meant I had to feed her more often throughout the day. Sometimes, I gave her a bottle to supplement so she could get enough milk.

I had heard some about the problems a tongue and lip tie can cause. I thought maybe our baby has a tie, and that is causing her difficulty in breastfeeding. So we went to get an evaluation for her. According to the pediatric dentist, she had a tongue, lip, and cheek tie. While the ties weren't major, they were just bad enough to cause her feeding problems. After the frenectomy, her feeding problems gradually improved. Then, I could breastfeed her until she was a year and a half.

My advice to other parents would be that if your baby is having feeding issues, it would be worth it to get an evaluation. If your baby has a mouth tie, a frenectomy can make a difference.

Rosi Yoder

# Final Thoughts

CONGRATULATIONS, YOU'VE REACHED THE end of this book. Hopefully, you've found many helpful tips along the way. You might have concluded that some things I outlined might not work for you and your baby–and that is fine. Each of us is embarking on a unique journey through motherhood.

I'd like to conclude with this message: you are a wonderful mother, and you are doing the best you can for your baby. Motherhood comes with many responsibilities, and taking care of a baby requires a lot of effort. So, even if you take away nothing else from this book, remember this — **you are an amazing mother.**

# Note From The Author

Update from Beth

Since my article for "Keepers At Home" has been published, I have had moms reach out to me for help for their older children. So, there's a couple of things that are important for you to know. First, a child from the age of three and up needs myofunctional therapy first. This includes adults. This therapy is critical because if the tongue has been tied down for a long time, it will become weakened. Then it is very important that you don't rush to get a release until exercises have been done for the tongue to strengthen it first. This is where myofunctional therapy comes in. So, you need to be sure that you find a knowledgeable dentist who understands the importance of doing myofunctional therapy first. If they do not recommend any therapy for the tongue before and after a release, I suggest you look elsewhere.

As these moms have been reaching out to me, I have been realizing that several specialists that are on the link that I provided are not recommending myofunctional therapy first, and I've really had to do a lot of searching to find not only good dentists for an older child but also a good myofunctional therapist. It is critical if you want the release to be done properly that you hire the right people to do it. The way I understand it is, myofunctional therapists don't need to take any training on how to help the tongue function properly and prepare it for a tongue tie release.

However, the fantastic ones who are committed and strive for excellence will take more training to learn this, so be very careful. Just a couple of weeks ago I was helping a client, and her baby was 15 months old, and the dentist recommended waiting until the child is three to do a release but said nothing about doing myofunctional therapy. This dentist was from the link I included in this book. I have been disappointed with some of these dentists. There are some fantastic dentists out there, and I have found that if you can find a knowledgeable dentist, they will recommend a skilled myofunctional therapist. In fact, the excellent dentists will actually have a myofunctional therapist in their office as well. If the dentist does not understand the need for myofunctional therapy first for a child this age or older, it's best to avoid them altogether and find a dentist that does.

Another thing to consider is that if you have a toddler, it is really, really difficult to do a release on them because of the specific age they're at. There is no toddler on the planet who likes to have someone mess around in their mouth. Not only that, once the release has been done, you need to do the stretches for the next three to six weeks, and your child is gonna fight you. Then what can happen is the stretches do not get done correctly, and then you would have been better off not having done the release at all. So, in this case, it is often a good idea to just wait until the child is closer to two or even three because then the child can understand what is going on, and it is less traumatic.

One question I get repeatedly is, "Do I **really** need to get my baby's ties corrected? What happens if I just let it go?" I understand it seems like a hassle, because I have been there. Here's what my advice is to you. Ask yourself this question: "What do I want to deal with later?" Let me explain.

My husband had chronic migraines for several years. He lived on ibuprofen to deal with the constant pain. As I began to learn about tongue ties because of my baby's issues, we suspected a tongue tie in him as well. He went through myofunctional therapy first, and then he got a tongue-tie release.

He said the relief he felt immediately after the release was incredible. He came out of that dentist's office a migraine-free man, and his migraines are a thing of the past. That was 3 years ago. What is interesting though, when he was a baby, his mom dealt with various symptoms I described in Chapters 11-12. Of course, she was not aware of the ties or their affects on her baby. When he grew out of the baby stage, the symptoms changed. However, no matter the symptoms, the oral restriction remained, along with his migraines, until a release was performed. Imagine how different his life would have been if this had been corrected when he was a baby? He would not have had to deal with intensely painful migraines for all these years.

If you don't correct this problem in the baby stage, some common symptoms a child will get are bedwetting, ADHD like behavior, difficulty concentrating, constant disruptive behavior, ear infections, swollen tonsils and/or adenoids, teeth grinding, restless sleeping, tooth decay, nightmares, and of course, muscle tension and headaches. These symptoms are considered normal but they are all an indicator of poor oxygen to the brain affecting a child's behavior (like ADHD like behavior, difficulty concentrating, and constant disruptive behavior) mouth breathing, (like swollen tonsils and/or adenoids, teeth grinding, restless sleeping, tooth decay) or restriction in the body (like bedwetting, teeth grinding, etc.) The reality is, ignoring ties does not make them go away. Sure, your baby will grow out of the baby stage, and eventually their sleep might improve a little. However, a baby, child or adult never grows out of a tie, and new symptoms will pop up as a result. There's a link below for an episode that covers bedwetting, ADHD, mouth breathing, and tongue ties from airway, jaw development, and sleep expert, Dr. Ben Miraglia.

At 8:54 *he starts talking about bedwetting, at* 17:39 *he covers ADHD, at* 43:53 *he dives into tongue ties*

I have worked some with older children and even 16-year-olds, and everyone of those parents tells me the same thing: "Oh, if **only** we had known this when he/she was a baby and would have corrected it then!" These children and their parents have suffered for years, just like my husband did, not knowing what the problem was. In fact, one mom who reached out to me has a child dealing with constant tonsil infections to the point where the doctor wants to remove them. Thankfully, she was aware there was a deeper problem and reached out to me. The problem is, the dentist and myofunctional dentist I recommended in her area don't have an opening for a couple more months. In the meantime, she is struggling to keep the tonsil infections under control. Could she go and have them removed? Absolutely, but the root cause is a tongue tie and a narrow airway from years of poor tongue function, and she knows this is just a symptom. Removing the tonsils would fix absolutely nothing, and her child would struggle with other symptoms because of tongue restriction. She is wise to wait and treat the root cause. Of course, if the tonsil infections become serious or life threatening, I would definitely have them removed for the sake of the child, but I would definitely follow up with myofunctional therapy and an evaluation from a tongue tie specialist. To learn more about why a narrow airway and/or tongue ties can cause swollen tonsils and infections in the tonsils or adenoids, I suggest finding Dr. Ben Miraglia online and listening to his videos. His website is called airwayhealthsolutions.com, and he's on Instagram @drbenmiraglia. I will include the link below for his podcast on Spotify, where he shares his expertise on inflamed tonsils, adenoids, mouth breathing, etc. and why simply removing the tonsils when a child is mouth breathing can be detrimental to a child's health. I have personally communicated with him, and he understands this issue better than I do. He has over 30 years of experience and is a trailblazer and an expert in the subject. You can also contact him through Instagram for further assistance in resolving these issues.

**Dr. Miraglia's podcast on jaw development and swollen/infected tonsils/adenoids**

*At 17:58 in the podcast, he talks about inflamed tonsils and adenoids*

As I mentioned before, the tongue determines the size of the jaw. When the tongue reaches to the top of the baby's mouth, it widens the jaw. A tongue is supposed to rest on the roof of the mouth. The problem with a tongue tie is, this is impossible. The result is a narrow jaw and crowded teeth. Nowadays, myofunctional therapists will sometimes recommend expanders to remedy this. Another thing to consider is, the longer you wait, the more intervention is needed to undo improper jaw growth and the more you will need to pay to fix it later. By the time you pay for myofunctional therapy, expanders, and a tongue and lip tie release, you can sometimes pay upwards of $6,000.00, with most of that cost coming from the expanders. If you take care of this as a baby, you will have much less cost involved, because less intervention is needed. As Dr. Ben Miraglia explains so well in one episode above, **"You could treat the cause early, or you will treat the symptoms forever."**

To understand the impact of tongue and lip ties on your child, and the optimal way to treat them, I suggest finding these talented experts online and listening to their podcasts.

1. Dr. Mandeep Johal. Her website is drmandeepjohal.com and her Instagram is @drmandeepjohal

2. Dr Mark Levi at dr.levis.com and on Instagram @drmarklevi and on YouTube at Dr. Mark Levi.

There are many more who are skilled in topics like airway health and tongue ties. There are many great myofunctional therapists on Instagram and online who can teach you so much about the impact of ties on your child's health.

Another problem that moms deal with frequently is that some dentists who don't have the proper training cannot identify and correct a posterior tongue tie. I am looking for specific training so that they not only understand oral function but also airway health. Many dentists don't have this specific training, and they will often tell moms that their baby has a lip tie, but no tongue tie when they simply don't have the expertise to identify a posterior tongue tie.

I had a mom who was having sleep issues with her baby, where her baby was waking up every hour during the night and she was exhausted. (I have seen many babies that only take short cat naps and wake constantly at night, and they all had tongue and lip ties causing this issue. Many of my clients see a tremendous difference in their baby's ability to sleep long periods of time after revising both the tongue and lip tie.) I recommended her going to a specific dentist with the proper training. However, she disregarded my advice and went to a lactation consultant. (It is really hard to find a lactation consultant, even an IBCLC (International Board Certified

Lactation Consultant) that has training to identify tongue and lip ties properly.) The lactation consultant recommended her going to a dentist that I knew nothing about. I had no clue what training he had or if it was the proper training that would help him diagnose and correct this baby's ties. The problem was, after she went to the dentist that the LC recommended, the dentist only identified and corrected the lip tie. A little later, she got back with me and said her baby was still not sleeping well and he was also choking a lot. So I knew there was still something going on and the baby likely still had a tongue tie, because tongue ties can cause a lot of choking. That's when she told me she never went to the dentist I recommended. So, now she got another lactation consultant and, thankfully, this was actually a knowledgeable lactation consultant and she told her, "Your baby still has a posterior tongue tie." Then she got back to me, wondering if her baby's posterior tongue really needed to be corrected. I told her that if she wants her baby to sleep better, absolutely, the tie needs to be corrected and she has to go to a dentist that I recommend if she wants this resolved for good. She disagreed and told me she wants to go back to the same dentist again and ask him to correct her baby's tongue tie. She said she had spent $1000 already, and she didn't want to spend that on another dentist just to get the posterior tongue tie corrected. I strongly advised her not to go back because I knew if the dentist wasn't able to identify the posterior tongue tie at the first visit, he would not identify it now. **He did not have the proper training to identify a posterior tongue tie.**

Finally, when she tired of her baby's sleep issues and constant choking, she took my advice. I helped her find a dentist in her area from the link, and the posterior tongue tie was corrected. A couple of weeks later, she messaged me and told me that her baby had slept his first eight-hour stretch at eight weeks old. So her baby went from waking up every 1-2 hours at night to sleeping 8 hours after the release! So this is a fantastic story of why it is critical that you find a knowledgeable dentist only or you will set yourself up for failure. I cannot tell you the amount of times that moms come to me and they tell me they have been to a lactation consultant, a chiropractor, a dentist, you name it, and they have been told that their baby has a slight tie, but it's nothing to worry about. Or they're told there's no tie at all, so Mom should stop worrying. When these moms finally come to me and I help them find the right specialist and the tie is corrected, so many of these baby's sleep issues leave. I have seen babies start sleeping better overnight once these ties are corrected. This is why I want to make sure you find a good, knowledgeable dentist who has specific training so you don't waste your time and money like this mom did. And remember, your baby rarely has just a lip tie when there's sleep issues involved. If your dentist tells you this, I would get a second opinion, because there's a good chance they don't know how to identify a tongue tie. That's why they tell you there is none.

# Dentists Who Perform Frenectomies, Lactation Consultants, Cranial Therapists

Scan the QR code to find tongue tie specialists in your area. You can also refer to the list below. **Before driving out of state to find a specialist, be sure to use the QR code to find someone in your area.** *The list below is not exhaustive-just because a specialist's name is not on here does not mean they are not knowledgable. However, just because a specialist's name is on here does not guarantee their ability to properly identify and correct your baby's ties either. To the best of my knowledge, these specialists have all taken the proper training and are knowledgable. However, because I have not personally consulted with most of them, if you question their judgement or it does not line up with what I mentioned in this book, don't be afraid of getting a second or third opinion.*

Tongue Tie Specialists Near Me

## Kentucky

Pediatric Dentistry of Hamburg (3 locations)
2517 Sir Barton Way, #200
Lexington, KY 40509
(859) 543-2456


208 Bevins Ln,A
Georgetown, KY 40324
(502) 570-2829


Capitol Kids Dentistry
315 Leonardwood Dr, #5
Frankfort, KY 40601
(502) 699-2571


Richmond Smile Design
311 Radio Park Drive Suite B
Richmond, KY 40475
859-623-3818
Fax: 859-624-1061

The Knapp Clinic
400 E. Main Ave. STE 309
Bowling Green, KY 42101-6900
Phone: (270) 697-9174
E-Mail: Support@KnappClinic.com
Phone: (270) 697-9174

## Georgia

Tongue Tie Center of Atlanta (I have personally communicated with the doctor here and he is very knowledgable and has an entire team including a lactation consultant. He has a lot of good content on Instagram @tonguetiecenteratl

400 Embassy Row NE, Suite 150
Sandy Springs, GA 30328
(470)-437-4337
Fax: 470-437-4334
info@tonguetiecenteratl.com

## Missouri

Center for TMJ and Sleep Apnea
3320 NE Ralph Powell Rd
Lee's Summit, MO 64064
(816) 795-1000


Springfield Kid's Dental
1802 W. Kearney St.,
Springfield, MO 65803
417-567-8227

The Abeille Feading Clinic (Very knowledgable crew here including a lactation consultant, SLP, myofunctional therapy, cranial sacral therapy, and tongue tie experts

11777 Gravois Rd.,
St. Louis, MO 63127
314-252-0153

The SLP here called Kayla Richardson, also does virtual consultants. Contact her by scanning the QR code below or going to bio.site/feedingbabystl

**Kayla Richardson website**

### Kansas

Kansas City Tongue Tie Co.
10058 Woodland Road
Lenexa, KS 66220
Phone: 913-800-2480

Krause Dental Center

9401 Nall Ave,
Overland Park, KS 66207
(913) 642-7272
Fax (913) 642-4434
Email contactus@krausedental.com

KC Dental Works
12705 West 87th Street Pkwy,
Lenexa, KS 66215,
(913) 432-9414
kcdentalworks@gmail.com

Herre Holistic Dental of Kansas City
11201 Nall Avenue, Suite 120
Leawood, KS 66211
913-491-4466
Email info@holisticdentalkc.com

Fetzik Dentistry
2548 N Maize Court, Suite 100
Wichita, Kansas 67205
(316)-440-4432

Cedar Lodge Dental Group
1001 Cody Avenue,
Hays, KS, 67601
785-625-7369

## **Colorado**

Colorado Tongue Tie
4704 Harlan Street #340
Denver, CO 80212
(720) 507-0077
https://www.coloradotonguetie.com


Falcon Pediatric Dentistry
11555 Meridian Market View,
Falcon, CO 80831
(719) 749-9001
Email info@falconpediatricdentistry.com


Thrive Growth and Development
15455 Gleneagle Dr., Ste 100
Colorado Springs, CO 80921
(719) 354-2472


Integrative Dental of Denver
771 Southpark Drive Suite #100,
Littleton, CO 80120
303-797-0832
Fax number: 303.797.0870


Balanced Dental Studio
7373 West Jefferson Ave, Unit 104
Lakewood, CO 80235
303-989-3192
Email hello@balanceddentalstudio.com

## Ohio

Brunswick KiDDS Pediatric Dentistry (*Brunswick KiDDS Pediatric Dentistry also has a YouTube channel called Brunswick KiDDS Pediatric Dentistry. If you go to the search bar and type in Brunswick kidds pediatric dentistry tongue ties, you can see videos they posted about mouth ties. There is a lot of helpful information and testimonies on their channel. Dr. Eilish is at this practice and is very knowledgable. I have communicated with her numerous times and consider her one of the best tongue tie specialists out there.*)

1824 Pearl Rd.
Brunswick, OH 44212
(330) 220-6363
https://www.brunswickkidds.com
Email smile@brunswickkidds.com


Dental and Cosmetic Solutions
3550 Lander Rd #140,
Cleveland, OH 44124
(216) 292-3600


Tiny Teeth of Dublin Pediatric Dentistry
5699 Innovation Dr.
Dublin, OH 43016
(614) 215-9488
Email info@tinyteethofdublin.com
https://www.tinyteethofdublin.com


Infant Lip/Tongue Tie Clinic
4834 Socialville-Fosters Rd ste 30 c,
Mason, OH 45040

513-459-1377

keely@masonelitedentistry.com

Chris Coleman DDS

1020 Franklin Rd.

Waynesville, OH

513-897-2001

Email office@chriscolemandds.com

Dentistry 4 Kids

3523 Commercial Dr.

Fairlawn, OH 44333

(330) 668-9977

https://www.dentist4kidz.com

Beckett Dental Care

8300 Princeton - Glendale Road, Suite 203

West Chester, Ohio 45069

 (513) 870-0700

Fax: (513) 870-0752

Email: appointments@beckettdentalcare.com

Breathe Dental

7729 Montgomery Road,

Cincinnati, OH, 45236

513) 857-3050

Email bewell@breathecincinnati.com

Little Ones Pediatric Dentistry

1600 W Lane Ave #150,
Upper Arlington, OH 43221
(614) 602-5004


Great Beginnings Pediatric Dentistry
9964 Vail Drive, Suite 1
Twinsburg, Ohio 44087
330-425-1885
Email Info@greatbeginningspd.com


Scott Dental Group (2 locations)
633 North Union Street
Loudonville, OH 44842
419-994-3111
Fax 419-994-4078


178 East Milltown Road
Wooster, OH 44691
330-345-7100
Fax (330) 345-6428


**Lactation Consultant**

Michelle Emanuel IBCLC
114 Wellington Place
Cincinnati, OH 45219
513-404-7786 (this says to text her here. I don't have any other
phone number for her besides this.

EmanuelOT@yahoo.com

# Pennsylvania

East Berlin Smiles (*At East Berlin Smiles they also have a* **lactation consultant** *and* **cranial therapist** *on staff. Very knowledgable.*)

418 West King Street
East Berlin, PA 17316
(717) 259-9596
https://www.eastberlinsmiles.com


Valley Pediatric Dentistry (3 locations)
(717) 253-9839


Harrisburg Office
4601 Devonshire Rd,
Harrisburg, PA 17109


Camp Hill Office
201 St Johns Church Rd,
Camp Hill, PA 17011


Carlisle Office
701 S West St,
Carlisle, PA 17013


Total Health Dentistry (2 locations)
524 Washington Street
Huntingdon, PA 16652
(814) 644-7128

616 4th Street
Altoona, PA 16602
(814) 944-1300


Buehler Family Dental
912 W Main Street Suite 404
New Holland, PA 17557
717-656-0005
Email info@buehlerfamilydental.com


Philadelphia Pediatric Dentistry
2000 Hamilton ST. STE 304
Philadelphia, PA 19130
(267) 440-7681


Westtown Dental Arts
1646 West Chester Pike, Suite 1,
West Chester, PA 19382
(610) 590-4568


Lesavoy Pediatric Dentistry (they have referrals for lactation consultants, SLP's, pediatric chiropractors, etc, and seem quite knowledgable)

1150 Glenlivet Drive, Unit C40,
Allentown, PA 18106
(610) 894-7544

Growing Smiles Main Line Pediatric Dentistry
701 Montgomery Avenue, Suite 2,
Narberth, PA 19072
610-890-7152
info@growingsmilesmainline.com


Infant Laser Dentistry
2301 East Allegheny Avenue Suite 201
Philadelphia, PA, 19134
info@infantlaserdentistry.com
(215) 282-9901


Laser Center for Pediatric Frenectomies (2 locations/doctors)

Gregory Lane, DMD
4623 State Route 136
Greensburg, PA 15601
(724)205-9610


Keith Gjebre, DMD
510 Pellis Road
Greensburg, PA 15601
(724)205-9610


Steel City Pediatric Dentistry
409 Broad Street, Suite 101-B - Sewickley, PA 15143
(412) 275-5406
steelcitypediatricdentistry@gmail.com

## Cranial Sacral Therapist, SLP, Lactation Consultant, Myofunctional Therapist

Ameera Therapy (2 locations)
Main office:
137 West Bridge St
Homestead, PA 15120

8620 Duncan Avenue
Pittsburgh, PA 15237
412-204-6641

## Cranial Therapists

Primary Care Services
991 Park Avenue
Meadville, PA 16335
(814) 373-1633

Cranial Sacral Fascial Therapy
Gladys Graybill
Meadville, PA
(814) 720-1739

Pain & Sleep Therapy Center – 2 locations, other location is listed below in Delaware

1149 Lancaster Avenue, Unit 5
Bryn Mawr, PA 19010
(610)819-7933

## Delaware

Pain & Sleep Therapy Center
620 Churchmans Road, Suite 203
Newark, DE 19702
(302)496-6072


Collins Dental and Orthodontics
38 Peoples Plaza,
Newark, DE 19702
(302) 834-4000

## Indiana

Wiley Green, DDS Holistic Dental
1961 S Jackson St.
Frankfort, IN 46041
765-659-3078


TMJ & Sleep Therapy Centre of Northern Indiana (2 locations)

7221 N. Fir Road,
Granger, IN 46530
574-968-5166


TMJ & Sleep Therapy Centre of Northern Indiana (I have personally visited their office and communicated with both the dentist and the myofunctional therapist here. They are my top recommendation for Indiana, because of their compassion and expertise. They use BabyLase here and cover all the bases of relieving oral tension in babies besides just releasing ties. When I was there, they gave me recommendations for a lactation consultant and a physical therapist that does cranial/fascia release in the area. I will put that information below.)

9914 Illinois Road,
Fort Wayne, IN 46804
260-387-6670

## Lactation Consultant

Danielle Henderson, IBCLC
(419) 934-5577

## Cranial/Physical Therapist

Dr. Jen Tippman
3110 Mallard Cove Ln.
Fort Wayne, IN 46804
(260) 431-8198

Mahoney Family Dentistry
17901 Turner's Drive
South Bend, IN 44635
(574)-272-0466
https://www.mahoneydds.com

Jansen Family Dentistry
230 South Main St.
Kendallville, IN 46755
(260)-347-5115
Email jansenfamilydentistry@gmail.com

http://www.jansenfamilydentistry.com

Newman Family Dentistry (2 locations) (*We do not recommend this office if your child is over one because of their anesthesia practices.*)

10425 Commerce Drive Suite 130
Carmel, Indiana 46032
(317)-218-9102

3945 Eagle Creek Parkway, Suite A
Indianapolis, IN 46254
(317)-451-4314
https://www.newmanfamilydentistry.com

Braces for all ages (2 locations)

3204 Lancer Street Suite A.
Portage, IN 46368
(219)762-5506
Fax (219)762-3870

186 Professional Court
Hebron, IN 4634
(219)996-7506
Fax (219)996-6635

**Cranial Therapists**
Speech, Feeding, and More

8202 Clearvista Parkway
Indianapolis, IN 46256
(317) 576-4764
https://www.speechfeedingandmore.com


Health Solutions for Life
625 E. Bristol Street
Elkhart, IN 46514
(574) 262-4402

## Michigan

Centerville Family Dentistry
664 E Main St #F
Centreville, MI 49032
(269) 895-6791


Pediatric Dentistry of East Lansing
3511 Coolidge Rd
East Lansing, MI 48823
(517) 337-0032
Email Office@yourchildsdds.com


Discover Smiles Pediatric Dentistry
2187 Jolly Rd Suite A,
Okemos, MI 48864
(517) 574-4688


Northwest Dental Excellence
1500 Parnall Rd

Jackson, MI 49201
Phone: (517) 513-8070
Fax: (517) 795 - 2687

Life Smiles Pediatric Dentistry
2775 E. Grand River Ave., Suite 3
Howell, MI 48843
(517) 518-8620

Ogemaw Family Dentistry
203 North 5th Street
West Branch MI 48661
989-312-3110

Mitten Kids Dentistry
6477 Cherry Meadow DR SE #4
Caledonia, MI 49316
(616) 942-9840
https://www.mittenkids.com

**<u>Cranial Therapist</u>**
Rambling Road Family Wellness and Chiropractic
2021 Rambling Road
Kalamazoo, MI 49008
(269) 381-1800

**<u>Iowa</u>**

The Children's Dental Center

2761 Oakdale Blvd, Suite 4
Coralville, IA 52241
319-626-KIDS (5437)
Email frontdesk@tcdcia.com

Des Moines Pediatric Dental Center
4949 Westown Parkway Suite 150
West Des Moines, Iowa 50266
(515)-225-0066
https://www.iowapediatricdentalcenter.com

Exceptional Dentistry of the Tri-State Region
4200 Asbury Rd.
Dubuque, Iowa 52002
(563)-556-2711
https://www.triexceptional.com

Anderson Dental
141 East 46th Street,
Davenport, IA, 52806
563-355-2010

Dental Touch Associates
5945 Council St.
Cedar Rapids, IA 52402
 319-519-4339

## New Jersey

Dayspring Dental

428 Ganttown Rd,
Sewell, NJ 08080
(856)875-8400


Tender Smiles 4 Kids (5 locations)

122 Professional View Drive Building 100
Freehold, NJ 07728
732-625-8080


1330 How Lane
North Brunswick, NJ 08902
732-249-1010


1656 Oak Tree Road
Edison, NJ 08820
732-549-3773


2209 N. Wood Ave.
Roselle, NJ 07203
908-245-5556


105 Berkeley Ave
Ocean Township, NJ 07712
732-774-7008


Pediatric Smile Works Dentistry
150 N. Finley Avenue Suite 101,

Basking Ridge, NJ 07920

(908)340-4848

## Illinois

Brimfield Family Dentistry

232 E. Knoxville St.

Brimfield, IL 61517

(309) 315-3623

https://www.brimfieldfamilydentistry.com

Cornerstone Family Dentistry

521 West Wall St.

Morrison, Illinois 61270

(815)-400-9141

https://www.midwestcornerstone.com

Grins on Green Bay (2 locations)

632 Green Bay Rd

Kenilworth, IL 60043

847-728-0030

Grins Highland Park

332 Skokie Valley Road , Suite 222

Highland Park, IL 60035

847-861-0030

## Montana

Alpine Family Dental

101 Westview Pk Pl.
Kalispell, MT 59901
(406)-393-8877
https://www.alpinefamilydentalmt.com


Rimrock Pediatric Dentistry (4 locations with 4 different names)

1601 Zimmerman Trail STE 1,
Billings, MT 59102
(406) 248-3303


Glasgow Pediatric Dentistry
54253 US-2 Suite A,
Glasgow, MT 59230
(406) 238-1200


Trailhead Pediatric Dentistry
513 Hilltop Rd Suite 5,
Billings, MT 59105,
(406) 500-8663


Beartooth Pediatric Dentistry
714 1st Ave ste 2, Laurel, MT 59044
beartooth@backbonedental.com
(406) 743-2327

## Alabama

Alabama Tongue Tie Center
2480 Pelham Pkwy

Pelham, AL 35124
(205) 419-4333
https://www.tonguetieal.com

## **Wisconsin**

Dental Kidds Pediatric Dentistry and Orthodontics (4 locations)

RIVERDALE KIDDS
3585 124th Ave NW, Suite 400
Coon Rapids, MN 55433
763-767-1524

ST. CROIX KIDDS
400 2nd Street S Suite 250
Hudson, WI 54016
(715) 808-0460

BLAINE KIDDS
1351 113th Ave NE Suite 400B
Blaine, MN 55434
(763) 415-1222

NEW RICHMOND KIDDS
1244 North Fourth Street, Suite 300
New Richmond, WI 54017
(715) 248-2246

Untethered Tongue Tie Center (2 locations)
2524 E. Webster Pl #201A

Milwaukee, WI 53211

414-935-8460 (text or call)

20350 Water Tower Blvd Suite 202

Brookfield, WI 53045

(414) 928-8877

hello@untetheredttc.com

BKS Dental

201 Sherman Avenue W

Fort Atkinson, WI 53538

920-563-7323

Email: team@bksdental.com

Center for Dentistry and Orthodontics,

Dr. Gerald S. Walczak

5625 Woodland St.

Stevens Point, WI 54482

(715)-341-8335

Email drgerry@charter.net

https://www.drwalczak.com

Smiles in Motion Pediatric Dentistry (2 locations)

840 Bear Paw Ave.

Rice Lake, WI 54868

(715)-723-2000

https://www.sim4kids.com

583 Lakeland Drive
Chippewa Falls, WI 54729
(715)-723-2000


Family Dentistry of West Salem
210 Leonard St. North,
West Salem, WI, 54669,
(608) 786-1632


Highland Dental and Fort Family Dental
1530 Doris Dr,
Fort Atkinson, WI 53538
920-563-9373
Email team@fortfamilydental.com


Spring Valley Dentistry (they are very knowledgable)

W502 State Rd 29,PO Box 190
Spring Valley, WI 54767
715-778-5543


Little Sprouts Dental
W65N640 Saint John Ave
Cedarburg, WI 53012
(262) 297-0079

### Maryland

Marcus Roberts, DDS
409 Main St.

Reisterstown, MD 21136
(410) 526-5050


Rockville Pediatric Dental
121 Congressional Lane, Suite 500
Rockville, MD 20852
(301) 881-0220
https://www.rockvillepediatricdental.com


Dentistry 4 Children (6 locations)
8600 Snowden River Pkwy,Suite 302
Columbia, MD 21045
410-941-3687

2 Hamill Rd.
Suite 266
Baltimore, MD 21210
301-603-3284


2410 Evergreen Road
Gambrills, MD 21054
410-701-3595


13600 Baltimore Avenue
Suite 200
Laurel, Maryland 20707
301-691-4620

50 Olney Sandy Spring Rd.

Ashton, MD 20861
301-259-3183


9812 Falls Rd.Suite 118
Potomac, MD 20854
301-281-6719


## Lactation Consultant

*Lactation Room (2 locations in Maryland, 2 in Virginia, at both Maryland offices, there is a cranial therapist as well)*

1 Park Avenue, Suite 1B
Mount Airy, MD 21771
(301) 529-5433
https://www.lactationroom.com


## Cranial Therapist

Nikki Clarke
(same address)
(443) 452-7524,
Email nikkiclarkecommunicationservices.com
*For scheduling, you can either call the main office at (301) 529-5433*
   *or contact Nikki at (443) 452-7524*
2nd lactation consultant office
1119 Rockville Pike, Suite 400
North Bethesda, MD 20852


## Cranial Therapist

Beth Willis
(same address)
*Call the main office to schedule an appointment at (301) 529-5433*

## Virginia

## Lactation Consultant

Lactation room (2 locations)
708 Pine Street
Herndon, VA 20170
(301) 529-5433


3859 Plaza Drive
Fairfax, VA 22030

Browning Family Dentistry
1151 13th St.  Ste. 200
Waynesboro, VA 22980
(540)-943-4215
https://www.bcfamilydentistry.com

## New York

Little Jaws Big Smiles
4605 E Genesee St.
DeWitt, NY 13214
(315)-299-4681
https://www.littlejawsbigsmiles.com


Untied Dental
310 East Court St.

Ithaca, NY 14850
(607)-882-0352
https://www.untieddental.com


Lawrence A. Kotlow, DDS, PC (Dr. Lawrence is very knowledgable)

340 Fuller Rd.
Albany, NY 12203
(518)-489-2571
https://www.kiddsteeth.com
Email drannie@kidsteeth.com


Winning Smiles Orthodontic, Pediatric, and General Dentistry (3 locations)

3476 Sheridan Dr
Amherst, NY 14226
(716)332-2444


205 Linwood Ave
Buffalo, NY 14209
(716)332-2444


3364 Southwestern Blvd
Orchard Park, NY 14127
(716) 332-2444

## Tennessee

Crestview Dental (I have personally communicated with a tongue tie specialist at this office, Tommy Spears. They are very knowledgable.)

1850 Crest Road
Maryville, TN 37804
(865) 982-1700
https://www.maryvilledentists.com

Paige Prather General and Holistic Dentistry (Dr. Paige Prather has over 10 years experience and is an expert)

3326 Aspen Grove Dr STE 120,
Franklin, TN 37067
(615) 709-5992

Children's Dentistry of Chattanooga
1612 Gunbarrel Rd., Suite 102,
Chattanooga, TN 37421
(423) 954-9511

Columbia Dental Group
1514 Hatcher Lane,
Columbia, TN 38401
931-381-7591

Allied Pediatrics (2 locations)
7405 Shallowford Road, Suite 270
Chattanooga, TN 37421
(423) 602-9545

https://www.myalliedpediatrics.com

5564 Little Debbie Pkwy, Suite 114
Ooltewah, TN 37363

Up Pediatric Dentistry
2829 Columbine Pl,
Nashville TN 37204
(615)440- 5188

Spring Creek Pediatric Center (Tongue Tie Center of Clarksville)

2698 Townsend Court Suite A
Clarksville, TN 37043
931-648-9930

Volunteer Pediatric Dentistry (2 locations)
1516 Coleman Road Suite 201
Knoxville, TN 37909
865-558-8857

209 East Emory Road Suite 101
Powell, TN 37849
865-512-9611

Morristown Pediatric Dentistry
950 West First North St.
Morristown, TN 37814

(423) 581-1877
Email: info@morristownpediatricdentist.com


Dickson Pediatric Dentistry
134 Highway 70 East
Dickson, TN 37055
615-740-8812


## Cranial Sacral Therapist

Melissa Star Craniosacral Therapist
1319 Old Weisgarber Rd.
Knoxville, TN 37909
lissamariposa@protonmail.com
(865) 387-0027


The Breathe Well Group (They offer cranial therapy as well as myofunctional therapy for all ages and serve MIDDLE TENNESSEE at these locations:

547 N Mt Juliet Rd suite 225, Mt. Juliet, TN 37122
1215 Lakeview Drive, Franklin, TN 37067
150 Uptown Square Ste B, Murfreesboro, TN 37129


ALSO SERVES WEST TENNESSEE
TeleHealth and Selmer, TN 38375
admin@thebreathewellgroup.com
Call:(615) 754-2134
Text:(615) 541-9249

Lactation Consultants

Nashville Birth and Babies (this is a group of lactation consultants)

Website nashvillebirthandbabies.com

**Phone:** 855-905-BABY (2229) Extension 3 - *If requesting an in-home visit, please state your location* when leaving a voicemail so to be paired with the home-visiting IBCLC that serves your particular neighborhood.

**Main Lactation Office:** The Sylvan Park office is located at 334 46th Avenue North, Unit A, Nashville, TN 37209 in side OMT of Nashville. This is a 2nd floor, home-like office in a historic building. There is no ramp or elevator access. If you have mobility/accessibility needs, please reach out to Kate at the email below to discuss your options.

Kate Cropp, MSN, APRN, WHNP, IBCLC
E-mail: kate@nashvillebirthandbabies.com


The Newborn Nurse (She serves the NASHVILLE • BRENTWOOD • FRANKLIN • NOLENSVILLE • MURFREESBORO • GERMANTOWN • GREEN HILLS • 12SOUTH • LEIPER'S FORK • SYLVAN PARK • SPRING HILL • BELLE MEADE • EAST NASHVILLE • THOMPSON'S STATION areas.

Email info@thenewbornnurse.com


Middle Tennessee Lactation (2 locations)
150 Uptown Square, Suite B

Murfreesboro, TN
*(Located inside Southern Mama's Chiropractic)*


161 Shirley Dr.
Winchester, TN 37398
*(The office of Amani Women's Health)*
615-785-7882
Email kimberly@middletnlactation.com


Tennessee Lactation Care LLC (She offers her services virtually as well as serving the south Nashville area including: Franklin, Thompson's Station, Spring Hill, Columbia, Nolensville, College Grove, Arrington, Eagleville, Chapel Hill, Lewisburg, Smyrna, Murfreesboro, Christiana, Bell Buckle, Shelbyville, and surrounding areas.

TennesseeLactationCare.com
(901) 568-9202


Hollie Stockdale (Jackson, TN)
(731) 616-1666

Nashville Lactation
Isabel Bennett IBCLC
(615) 583-9199
Email NashvilleLacation@yahoo.com


Ashley Lucas (Chattanooga, TN)
Ashley@chattanoogalactation.com
(423) 619- 3622

For The Love of Lactation (Serves Maryville, Greenback, Vonore, Alcoa, Lenoir City, Knoxville, & surrounding areas in East TN.)

(843) 276-9489
Email sarah@fortheloveoflactation.com

## Oregon

Dr. Ghaheri (2 locations) Dr. Ghaheri is an ENT turned tongue tie specialist and is very knowledgable. He has a lot of good content online on Instagram @drghaheri.

1111 NE 99th Ave, Suite 101
Portland, OR 97220
(503) 488-2626
https://www.drghaheri.com


24076 SE Stark, Suite 230
Gresham, OR 97030
(503) 488-2600

# Resources

## Organic Blackstrap Molasses

Organic Blackstrap Molasses

This code contains an affiliate link. If you make a purchase through this link, I will receive a commission.

## Blackstrap Molasses

Blackstrap molasses

This code contains an affiliate link. If you make a purchase through this link, I will receive a commission.

## Organic Cracked Cell Chlorella

Organic Cracked Cell
Chlorella

This code contains an affiliate link. If
you make a purchase through this link, I
will receive a commission.

## Deep Tissue Salve

Deep tissue salve

## Kefir Grains

The Kefir Lady Website

## Topical Magnesium Salve

# Junior's Bedtime Lotion

Junior's Bedtime Lotion

This code contains an affiliate link. If you make a purchase through this link, I will receive a commission.

# Doterra Diaper Rash Cream

Doterra Diaper Rash Cream

This code contains an affiliate link. If you make a purchase through this link, I will receive a commission.

# Redmond Bentonite Clay

Redmond clay powder

## NoseFrida the Snotsucker

NoseFrida the Snotsucker

This code contains an affiliate link. If you make a purchase through this link, I will receive a commission.

NoseFrida the Snotsucker
Travel Case

This code contains an affiliate link. If you make a purchase through this link, I will receive a commission.

NoseFrida the Snotsucker
With Saline Solution

This code contains an affiliate link. If you make a purchase through this link, I will receive a commission.

## The Booger Picker

The Booger Picker

This code contains an affiliate link. If you make a purchase through this link, I will receive a commission.

As mentioned in the book, both the NoseFrida and the Booger Picker are available from Target.

## Antibacterial Body Cloths

Norwex Antibacterial body Cloths

This code contains an affiliate link. If you make a purchase through this link, I will receive a commission.

## Herbs for Fever Solution/Ear Infection Formula

Mullein Flowers

This code contains an affiliate link. If you make a purchase through this link, I will receive a commission.

Lobelia Herb, Cut

This code contains an affiliate link. If you make a purchase through this link, I will receive a commission.

Chamomile Herb, Cut

This code contains an affiliate link. If you make a purchase through this link, I will receive a commission.

## Baby Probiotics

Baby Probiotics

SCAN ME

This code contains an affiliate link. If you buy a product with this link, I will get a commission.

Baby Probiotics

SCAN ME

This code contains an affiliate link. If you buy a
product with this link, I will get a commission.

# Notes

Concepts used with permission from Lawrence A. Kotlow, DDS, SOS 4 TOTS, second edition, 2017, Troy Book Makers; Troy, New York

# Also by Beth Miller

*Here's why this book has been a bestseller multiple times since release.*

As a mom of three, I know firsthand how challenging, exhausting, and painful labor can be. With my first two babies, **I endured long, grueling 24-hour and 18-hour labors-despite trying every natural remedy I could find,** from red raspberry leaf tea to herbal concoctions. Nothing seemed to shorten the labor or alleviate the pain.

*But everything changed when I got pregnant with my third baby.*

Determined to have a faster, less painful experience, I dove deep into research. What I discovered about regulating the hormones controlling labor and preparing my mind spiritually for birth was a game-changer. With these new strategies in place, I had a birth experience that was completely different. **This time my labor was 75% less painful, and my baby was born in just 3 short hours!**

**In this book, you'll learn:**

• The no.1 thing most moms miss that that can cut labor in half
• Tried-and-true strategies to help your baby align in the pelvis for optimal positioning for a quicker and easier birth.
• How your mind dictates how painful labor is
• How to equip your mind mentally and spiritually for the most painless labor possible

**This Book is For You If:**

• You want a faster, easier labor using proven, natural methods

- You're interested in reducing pain during contractions without drugs
- You want to prepare mentally and spiritually for the birth experience
- You want holistic, natural remedies for postpartum healing for both you and your baby

**This Book is NOT For You If:**

- You prefer traditional medical interventions over natural birth strategies
- You're looking for a quick fix and aren't willing to prepare your body and mind for labor
- You're not open to incorporating natural remedies into your birth and postpartum care
- You don't believe in God and prayer

*For three of my four children, I had 18-hour labors. But with one of my babies, labor was completely different-it only lasted 2 hours and 15 minutes. In fact, I believe I was in early labor for a number of hours without realizing it. Afterwards, I couldn't figure out why this labor was so much faster than my other births until I read this book. That's when everything clicked. I had a light bulb moment and realized there was one simple change I made during the last stretch of my pregnancy that made all the difference. It was such a minor change that I never even considered the possibility that it could have helped to dramatically shorten my labor, until this book explained the science behind it. Now I understand exactly why that one change change made my labor 600% faster.*

A MOM, PENNSYLVANIA

**To purchase this book, you can either contact the bookseller where you got this book, or scan the QR code below to purchase it directly from my publisher.**

*You can purchase "How to Have a Faster, Less Painful Natural Birth" by scanning this QR code with your smartphone.*

www.ingramcontent.com/pod-product-compliance
Lightning Source LLC
Chambersburg PA
CBHW051151120626
46547CB00012B/1046